TALES AND POEMS

BY LOUIS GRUDIN

AN EYE IN THE SKY

INKY DARKLING

A TEARLESS GLASS

A PRIMER OF AESTHETICS

MR. ELIOT AMONG THE NIGHTINGALES

THE OUTER LAND AND OTHER POEMS

CHARLATAN

IGNOMINY

TALES AND POEMS

LOUIS GRUDIN

Tales and Poems

HORIZON PRESS NEW YORK

TALES AND POEMS by Louis Grudin includes: *Ignominy,* a
narrative and a collection of new poems; three groups of
"transcriptions for voice" from the novel, *Inky Darkling,*
published by Dial Press in 1954; a new version of *An Eye
In The Sky,* Dial Press, 1960; and selected poems from
earlier books: *The Outer Land and Other Poems,* Dial
Press, 1951; *A Tearless Glass,* Covici, Friede, 1934; and
Charlatan, Lieber & Lewis, 1923.

Some of the poems first appeared in the following publi-
cations: *The Nation, The New Republic, The Forum, The
Little Review, Broom, Poetry* (Chicago), *The Chap Book*
(London), *The World Tomorrow, Rhythmus, Caprice,
Pagany, The American Caravan, The New Pocket Anthol-
ogy of American Verse* (World Publishing and Pocket
Books, Inc.), *Art Voices, Poet's Gold* (The Devin-Adair
Company) and *New Letters in America* (W. W. Norton).

FOR LILLIAN

CONTENTS

EARLIER POEMS

IGNOMINY

1

I LIE BREATHING the prisoner's air, dreaming in my noon-hour blindness, in the chill of the truth. What can I make of it, its mysteries and surprises? What can possibly appear of what has flamed away, or sailed out of sight with the last steamer of the old Ward line, or was carried off by a demolition crew with the Roman columns and breasty stone eagles of the vanished Penn Station, where now the concrete pile of the new Madison Square Garden is visible from my window?

Strangest of all, to have come in the end to this improbable place. Here, just off the fur district, I take my daily walk, west to the Hudson River docks or south to 20th Street or north to Times Square. To the east I enter an endless perspective of crumbling loft buildings, each with its dark hallway door and narrow store front window. Behind the glass a warped floor runs on and on into the rear where one might find an elderly man seated at a work table under a naked electric light. He is in his sixties, his eyes are pouched and lined, staring point blank like an old hippo. He is a furrier; he sorts and trims the pelts of little beasts. His face bears the marks of weakness, marks of woe. His is the trance of the sedentary for whom the ambulance siren will wail.

In the hallway the elevator shaft of a converted stairwell wears a black pushbutton on its open ironwork cage. The airless interior is spiked with erosion, the crazed wall weeps zones of acid seepage. It is an architecture of apathy, abandoned to decay, the unregarded rear of man's visible estate. Under its spell the old furrier's spirit cannot stir to as much as a sparrow's chirp.

Upstairs the small fur firms have their lofts, partitioned with panels of dark plywood and frosted glass, and eastward on Seventh Avenue are the more solid firms with their brass plaques and huge plate glass windows. One displays a dusty stuffed fox, another has a polar bearskin impaled on the wall. The legends on the glass touch off intimations of wilderness and arctic wastes, proclaiming in type of imitation gold: SEAL, OTTER, ERMINE, BEAVER, LEOPARD, SILVER FOX, BLACK MINK.

Do I have the courage to go out today, to the limits of my bounds? My flight from the past ended at the same point of departure and arrival, confirming once again that space is curved and returns upon itself. Actually it is only a short drive from the scene of what might have been my last take-off. I had made a wrong turn and shot uphill to a clifftop. If my car had not miraculously stalled I would have been airborne to the gulf and the rooftops suddenly in view below.

Very like the flights of some I have known who ventured beyond their depth, deluded amateurs, ambitious lunatics seduced by the charisma of one's own near and resonant word. Reminding me of misfortunes and the mysterious loss of friends. Not merely those whom one has outlived, who by their passing into irreparable absence assume an unforeseen endearment, but those who have abandoned and forgotten us, raising the painful perplexity of the failing self: what really happened?

There was one who wrote to me and healed me with his praise, an inspired comrade's gift of charity, from the wealth of his lucky genius. In what a panic once I heard him read a poem of mine! With sudden near-sighted concentration, line by line he retraced a stanza with his index finger, declaiming in his faint, hollow, melodious voice, nodding approval while I choked like one condemned:

When the silent woe is ripe
In fruit to fall,
It is then the private death
Becomes the funeral
And the one darkly struck down
Is visible to all.

Through the bitter cold down Ninth Avenue, my overcoat collar buttoned up close, my rubbers slippery over the hard packed snow, I reached the little bookshop where half the newly built shelves were still bare. Gabriel was to meet me there; he had waited and given up and gone home. I confess I was nearly an hour late, but I lingered to chat with the slack young man who ran the shop, because he asked me if any of my books were still in print.

I went on to Gabriel's and banged on his door without response. I was about to leave when it opened a crack and his small, withered, tight-lipped face peered fiercely through. "You could have telephoned," he said at last in his tender, mincing voice as he led me into the tiny living room and motioned to the one big easy chair. Soon, with rising eloquence, though still a bit testy and breathless, he was expounding his great work in progress, *The Galactic Origin of Man.*

It would grieve me to leave him here with this mere mention, as exasperating as a passport photo. In deference to the truth I have altered his name and the title of his masterpiece, and thus the dubious fact becomes its melancholy analogue, fiction.

In his warm, sweet, insistent way, his eyes dancing, a faint pink of old age fever in his cheeks, Gabriel convinced me to accompany him to the party at the Snark Bookshop. He had it all wrong of course. Martha, he said, had told him merely that there would be "a gathering of a few poets" at four thirty, and he argued that she surely would have asked me too if I had been around.

The spacious meeting room, a long flight up above the Snark Bookshop, was almost empty. On the open door in fine gold lettering: THE SHEM AND SHAWN CLUB. At the bar in a far corner, three lost elders stood clinging to their cocktail glasses. Two young men were still up on ladders, hanging the last of a number of photo-murals. A pretty girl, helpless with a yardstick and a hammer, introduced herself as a friend of Martha's from *Book News*. I knew one of the editors there. With a shock I remembered that after his wife died I was nearly a year late with my untimely letter of condolence, which in fact reached him on the eve of his remarriage.

Martha appeared in the doorway. Like the cockney flower girl in Shaw's *Pygmalion* she had made it to the big time. And now in her eightieth year and in the Snark's sixtieth, it was my luck to crash the anniversary party, to sign the guest book and win her brief hostess smile, an uninvited guest and, in accord with my anachronistic nature, to have arrived too early. But soon the guests would be crowding in and I would be crushed against a wall, the news cameras flashing, and just behind and above me, the group photomural made from a camera shot back in the early thirties at another Snark party, of the Sitwells, Edith and Osbert, and Auden and the Gregories and Sam Putnam and Delmore Schwartz and a few others, staring down at me from that other occasion.

Edging my way out, I paused to look at the Cummings self portrait on the corridor wall, surprisingly academic and as dainty as the flute-like cadences of his verse. Martha had not sent me the Snark announcement of their new art gallery which was to open with a show of his paintings, and this too was curious, that I was not on her list. The unanimity of estrangement from each and all, and once for all.

2

Emanuel had crossed the ocean and reached the stern and rock-bound shore. He had stood on a dreary Manhattan rim of weathered piers and slapping waves, where the ugly white gulls tossed high like fish hooked to their hunger. He was lost in the slum streets and the green plaster walls of the boxed darkness that awaited all who came by steerage; and moved on west to still another shore. No word from him until one winter night I saw him off on his way back to Italy, stooped, already balding, trembling in what was to be his terminal ague, helpless to light a cigarette. In the rear seat of a bus riding home I grieved for him over the driving wind and hissing wheels of Riverside Drive.

It was forty years later that I happened on a copy of his "Autobiography" in the little shop on Ninth Avenue. The misty photo on the book jacket, as flimsy as a fade-out on a movie screen, showed the wide brow, the brooding eyes, the abstract edge-line of the small, pursed mouth. Yes, it was Emanuel. He had passed into the calm of the abated storm, the peace of the resolved and legendary realm, where the vanished and remembered are. *"What Adonais is, why fear we to become?"* I paid for the book, hurried out with it to a lamp-lit doorway for a quick second look, and gasped to hear his voice, instant and near, from the random page. It was the Emanuel who had stood with me in the shadow of the Woolworth Building and had tramped with me all night through Central Park.

That was on my return from the U. of A., which had been run as a boot training camp by Texan leathernecks. There, on campus, in class and in the barracks, I had held my breath under the spell of the little white lies and the tight-drawn leers of the little old south'n foxes who showed their teeth to little old me, down yonder. Somehow whenever things are just beginning and there's a hint of promise in the air they pull a war on you. The present one is my fourth, you know, for I was that mangy private who came home from World War One.

> Caught a train to Times Square,
> fleeing south'n justice
> in sovereign Alabam, with my banjo
> and my bias in favor of color
> versus pallor.

Once on my way home from school I had noticed, high over the rooftops, something strange, a silvery glitter hovering near the early moon. It was what we had read about in the papers—a flying machine. That tiny throbbing wing in the sky was the lark at heaven's gate, the star of the East, the comet of awe-struck ancient man. There was only one other sight that rivalled it—a battleship motionless in the middle of the Hudson River, like a nightmare crocodile, a monstrous secret exposed by the early morning sun, a bristling exoskeletal steel cockroach, a stupefying herald of the impending War.

Emanuel was foreign, ragged, handsome, lively with vulnerable valor and self-mockery and alarmingly quick to anger. The sorrows of his book sparkle with crystal moments that shine like tears. Though he was a few years older than I, we shared a sublime impatience for Utopia, with no taint of doubt or hesitation. Somewhere he mentions my declaration that love is the only rational state. Could I really have been up to that exasperating Socratic presumption, could that dazzling hubris have lit up my green young self?

I was still in my baggy uniform, which I wore like a disease. Exaltation, prowess and humiliation were my daily fare, as they were Emanuel's. I was eighteen years old and had broken away from the parental tenement. I had found a half-day job and a hallway cell in a downtown rooming house. A group of my poems had been printed in a literary magazine. And why not? Was there ever a bum too poor for pen and paper, the runaway boy Rimbaud, the jailbird Villon, or Sam Greenberg in the garment district, who wrote a sublime sonnet which appeared in Hart Crane's book, *White Buildings* without acknowledgment? He died of T.B. in a slum hospital ward. Versed in misfortune, like Coleridge's albatross and Poe's anonymous raven and crazed, ruined young Crane who plunged from a steamer deck, his torment by fire extinguished in anguish by sea.

A raw browbeaten youth stranded in the streets and my sole possession a library card. A mouse in a china shop, where there was no sustenance, nothing edible, everything in Sanscrit; sitting by the hour in the same hovering spirit, captivated by the mysteries of the printed word. In a book on Logic I was snagged right off by the phrase: *"If so-and-so is the case . . ."* The absurdity of the assumption, the ineffable oddness of being the case, of being apparent and being intended and being there and being so-and-so, was just what baffled me and what I could not get beyond.

And one day I struggled with a cryptic verse in a small book of astounding bite and swaggering beat and was staggered by the line: *"All this our South stinks peace."* This must be the case and must be poetry too, for it was in verse and was printed in a book. And how utterly unlike the solemn sonnet I had recited in class at Townsend Harris Hall, *Milton On His Blindness,* a trite thing, I thought, for anything seemingly lucid and approved by my elders was a settled bore, lacking in the taunt of the unknown, of which I was apparently the given case, presumably by direct descent from an unimaginable Father, my pristine self being the premise of the universe, soon to be further befogged by the clever interlocutory voice of Berkeley, another of my bewildering encounters in the public library.

How huge and compelling, in those days, the things I saw and heard as a boy, in dumb shock, in that haze, in that distant air, now as visible as the sea. The past, far off like the childhood of the race, where we skipped in airs that hurt not. The past, in a kodachrome film slide viewer, where I saw, in radiant unearthly miniature, a long forgotten family party (myself among them) existing transfixed, around a festive dinner table.

Many a refugee from Czarist Russia
found asylum in my father's house.
One winter night
a quiet-breathing stranger at our table,
who touched the glowing glass with his palms
and sipped the fierce comfort of the scalding tea,
gave me a little book: *What's To Be Done?*
From the small print a voice arose
like hands clasped in entreaty;
the words were simple, fabulous and baffling,
like my father's friends seething in debate,
with ponderous eloquence and acid jest.
I frowned, sighed, tossed with each in turn,
in the rough weather of their worldly music.

And on many a rare hour I would stand
in my miracle of luck, among the stars,
in the brightness of being
which is the singing of the world,
and turn back to my narrow bed,
draw close the scant coverlet
and sleep in splendor's shade.

The other day I discovered that a character named Tevya, a long forgotten friend of my childhood, was appearing in a Broadway musical. When I had first met him, in a book by Sholem Aleichem (whose niece I think I once kissed, or very nearly did) I had cried and laughed out loud. I have a funny feeling of the imminence and readiness of tears. Again the precious tear: that was my heritage as their fargone kin in the free world. And it struck me that I had given my parentage little piety or thought. In fever and in rage, the moment I could flap a wing I flew the roost.

And this morning Sylvia brought me Malamud's new book of stories, *Idiots First.* "Before I return it," she said, "be sure to read *Black Is My Favorite Color,* the nicest story in the book." It was done with the mere crumbs of words, each morsel so dearly bought, and it made a feast. Never mind how, from his endowment of quiet health, of easy unflagging attention, steady and whole from his prophetic young heart as a poor fool wasting his substance on the silly forlorn hope of writing what?—and for whom?—and by whatever means, by the meanest and most meaningful means, among the innumerable voices in the world, writing a story like *Black Is My Favorite Color.*

The blast of a megavoice from a passing sound truck strikes terror, brays to the horizon and over. What was I saying? I thought I might make a go of it, with a little bit of luck, all in good time, in any light that showed, and have a look at my lifetime trip as a stranger and an adman; with a little gentle justice here and there, to each and all a hand-out of my time and place in history, for I've had it. The day has maybe come to do like Hirsch and surprise my friends with a little bounty from the blue.

3

Sylvia looked up from the new paperback of Alex Rosen's memoirs and said, "Listen to this about Else von Freitag von what was the rest of her name, did you know her?"

"Loringhoven," I said, "please don't go on, I couldn't take Alex today." It would be too much: the echo of his style of some four decades ago, his rapid cackle as his blurred eyes lit up in a happy glare, pausing open mouthed for applause, his wrinkled ornamental face with the sloppy hungarian moustache; his limp, diminished frame afloat in space, with still a sly tilt of the head. To listen to him once more, to lapse into savage Rosenian caricature, it would drag one back into a coarse-line halftone screen in yellow newsprint, with the shock effect of a fist to the face, coarsening the features, turning them into a lino alloy, a leaden dross disgrace. It would blacken the eye and the name, and swell the lip and bruise and batter the outline into a two-dimensional calumny.

How tired I am, from genesis to finisis, a pretty long time to hold one's breath. It was Charles Peirce who at the end of a long meditation noticed that he had been holding his breath, which fascinated him, for he was concerned with breath and soul, like Socrates, who was reputed to have had those trances when he turned as rigid as a diagram, standing a day and a night barefoot in the snow in a trench before Potidaea in the dead of winter.

To tell the truth I never did read all five volumes of Peirce's *Collected Papers,* a gift from a friend who later turned foe, a turnabout which to my dismay appears to have been the pattern of my past, whether on Skid Row or in the Vatican splendor of the publishing house where my friend Rock Cominsky sat owlish and amiable behind his enormous editorial desk. My coxie's army of friends turned foe: Alex and Archie, Myra and Gabriel and how many another, not to mention a certain young bitch scorned, who stole and destroyed my only draft of a book of poems, the fruit of a year of solitary labors.

And I was disenchanted with Santayana, now resident in a convent in Spain, in the foreign silence of the nunnery walls. To me, his dark glowing Spanish eyes are still as irremediably remote as they had ever been in the long fierce days of winter famine, of apple vendors on icy sidewalk corners, of Macarthur's horsemanship in the streets of Washington. He looked exactly like General Franco, the one whom our fat little American Cardinal in his piteous infant voice lauded and blessed as "that splendid Christian Gentleman."

Our dark saint in Franco's convent was on a perpetual sabbatical from America, like that other self-exile whose name shrinks from memory, that cranky envenomed Ezra who took shelter in Benito's steaming breast, far from sight or sound of the kin of my heart, the dear ones for whom my mother grieved, who were driven into the sealed freight cars.

Somehow angle by angle we'll zero in on what had been there and what was with them and with me. *"What's with you?"* was how Joel once greeted me when I called at his office. He would stand small and erect while his eye roamed and he enlivened his remarks with outrageous softly voiced curses and obscenities. Once at a gathering he astonished me by a sudden show of brutality to a total stranger; the minimal courtesy of silence should have cost him so little! He would rage without warning, like my friend Hirsch who had secretly left me a thousand dollars in his will, and decided (all unknown to me) to disinherit me, infuriated by my not too gentle remarks concerning the clownish gibberish of his pronouncements on Art. A near thing. And as erratic as little Joe Gould, "whose writing was uneven." All now absent. How would they shape up in the line-up, where once I fancied I might assemble them (as in a crime movie) where they would set each other off, in the open, in a Magritte effect, in unmitigated space, all lit up and everything showing?

That was when Everyman still loomed large and near, high on the horizon, in heroic line, in semblance of eternal meaning, where I saw friend and foe alike as big as Life, and myself reverberating with my favorite book, the tall red-bound *Romantic English Poetry* in double column pages of thin Bible paper. I can still see it in its place on my shelf, recalling my post-Whitman and pre-Joycean phases as a sweaty young vagrant and inky laborer, a darkling loiterer and solitary prowler, somehow surviving as a free lance hack by random art jobs.

> Pray sir, can you spare
> a farthing for a lad from the far hills
> where Wordsworth saw the old leech gatherer?

My office was just west of Brentano's where I once came face to face with a long lost friend hesitating before me in astonished recognition. Around the corner, Dan's father the dean of publishers once took me to lunch. And nearby to the south was the towering church of blackened stone, a citadel bristling with slotted battlements, where more than one old friend of mine had made his final departure from the scene.

Many a morning I would vanish down the corner subway entrance, to surface on Canal Street. There I would haunt the War Surplus stores and the machine shops along Center and Lafayette Streets. It was not far from Liberty and West where briefly I had worked in that other loft in the bygone mist, overlooking the docks and ships off the Hudson shore.

It was near the Photo Mart where once they picked my pockets in the darkroom and threw me out in the freeze without subway fare to my midtown office, where there was hardly more than elbow room to turn and reach for my pen, to jot down my name and address, just to make sure, just in case, and maybe just in time. It was jammed wall to wall with machine tools, stacks of drawings, and working models of my abandoned inventions, to which I would later refer as "my herd of white elephants," my jaunty way of beating disparagement to the punch.

Still free to go as I pleased, to emerge and pick up an achromat advertised in the Sunday Classified for my prototype of an automated phototypesetter, and how about that? What was I doing in that area, in types and graphics, illuminations and phanophonetics and phanolytics and epifannies, enmeshed in notions and motions and working models? Fitting parts to parts, male and female, refillable and interchangeable in Cybernia, region of cold fact.

Among my exploits was the colophon I designed for the Worldwide Library. In minimal outline like a watermark, it graced the title page of one of their earliest books, *Literature and Revolution*. A bit of evidence of participation, this public, anonymous, perishable mark, proof that once I did my part and partook and did indeed appear (a fateful secret firefly flicker) somewhere in the night of history.

A small paper sign scotch taped to the corner lamp post announced in staggered childish lettering: POETRY READING. 8.30 TONIGHT. FREE REFRESHMENTS. I decided to go and see, and there in the meeting hall I found at the podium an aged little man in a loose and spreading frame. It was Gabriel! His sharp old eyes danced in the shadow of tufted brows as jaunty as a macaw's crest. Their liveliness belied his voice of hovering sadness and breathless pauses as he presided over his little band of the poor in spirit. How many knew that his verses had once appeared in *The Criterion?* And why mention it now, well, just because it was there, a fact as sudden as the beep and toot of traffic that shot off and away to where all else had gone. And also because it was my reward for venturing once more from my apartment. Like my office downtown it was choked with my indescribable hoard of papers and lost causes and effects without title, key or index. All despite my philosophy of emergence and deliverance, such as is imaged in the primal rising from the sea, and in Noah's mission to endure the deluge, out-ride the gulf and out-reach the tide. It had been the faith of my youth, manifest to me in so many ways: even in the persistent redundancy of birth, in the ever-sudden recurrence of singular new being.

Becalmed now in my maximum security cell high above sea level, over the West Side flats, near the rotting wharves and the lapping water's edge, in a gigantic high-rise tenement, a rattling shell of cinder blocks and glass, in a moaning draft from the elevator shaft, twenty stories above the rumbling basement crypts. It was a myopic deafened immigrant garment-cutter's dream, as false as a fancy greeting card, of stately mansions, oh my blind-alley soul, to affright a visitor from outer space, who would flee this great roaring hive, back where he came from, in terror of earthlings and their things.

It had been a hard day. I had despaired over the Vietnam headlines, and had finished my black and white collage of a female figure in a leap over the horizon, a cyclone spiralling at her heels, her distant, sky-surrounded head (diminished in perspective to a black dot) crossing in eclipse the hieroglyphic eye of advancing night. This was accomplished in defiance of arthritis and acute scintillating scatoma, a blinding migraine. I had also run up a fever by indulging my sudden compulsion to dial everybody on my old list of friends whom I had not seen in years; cursing the wrong numbers, the no-answers and the busy signals to no avail; and that's how it went that day, how it danced and rattled and skipped into the past.

4

A rockaway, a crazy way of tossing and showing up, like poor Al Schiller on the telephone. A faint voicelet bore me the news by wavelet from his hospital bed, that he was feeling fine. On that same day the phone rang again, and Eve's cherry-fresh soprano sang in my ear that Jimmy Hardy had died.

Tidings of rough weather, and how explain it, the aptness of accident, the smack of the nearest wave, that happens to be just how it is, by incredible contingency, that brought me to such a pass. To be so engaged, on my cosmical course, a funny corsair, a discoverer, a missionary messiah, a woeful confessor to a world's end, to a misseh mishumeh, a false dawn's glimpse of a rockbound landing.

There as an immigrant child I had been abandoned to the rock of pilgrim's pride; and now, the grandsons of the grandsons are swamped in the orient land mass, full circle westward from East to East, following our star steadfast to a smoke-stack Fujiyama, symbol of peace, on the isle of our ally of forgotten infamy, in the free world of free will and original sin; our heads full of acid syllables, foul vocables, verminous words and rattling skies.

And we started it, we did! It was our atomic brilliance, our choice of cause and consequence undreamed-of in Elizabethan verse. Our Father who art in the White House! Ah, wilderness! (What was the name of the author of that play?—fogged out, and only the gaunt spectral face and frame of dear Sam Putnam, who resembled him.) Imagine forgetting that illustrious name, the father-in-law of Charlie Chaplin, and brother of all the strayed under the star, the cross, the pentad and the hex (of ill luck). Stranded on an alien shore. Eugene O'Neill of course, who also looked like solitary Sinclair Lewis with a bottle of cognac at a table in a Swiss café, his face flushed and disfigured somehow like a stage face of a Cyrano.

It would seem unthinkable, in an ever continuous universe of next-to-next, that one could reach a next-to-nowhere. And then it happens and there you are: a *ledig-gehr.* That was old Rovy's whimsical epithet for one who had retired, an *idle-goer.* He told me once gleefully how he would infuriate an old acquaintance with the witty greeting: *"Welcome to the club, ledig-gehr!"* I wonder at this trifling: am I echoing the fatuities of my elderly friends? "Carrying on," I tell myself, "bearing your being and your meaning still unknown to your odorous old self, maintain-

IGNOMINY   15

ing and manifesting yourself, as far as you go, an epiphane,
a sounding telephane, an echomantic."

A long way since, and all my causes lost,
on a pittance and a strand of silver hair,
my last-chance flyer on a fling:

To roll in the early grass
and spring to life a newborn colt
and toss my telltale and prance in the past,
to the smell of battle and the mare in the wind,
and a fade-away laugh
of faraway turf and track, and a short view
of the boneyard,
a crazy tune from where I stand,
hey nonnie and shed a tear.

Released and out on my feet on the street in my old
civilian clothes, five dollars in my pocket, a free man in the
Free World, without a job or a deadline, free of my strange
and bootless lifetime strain, what was it anyway? How come,
this single-mindedness to be, to stay on, like the President,
for another term, to scheme awhile longer, to ask myself:
signifying what? Simply, my long lost cause. And as to that,
I am reminded of an invalid friend of mine, a survivor of a
massive heart attack, who said: *"women! you can have
'em!"*—in the same voice as the doctor who took care of
my father in his nineties had exclaimed: *"old age, who
needs it?"*—shortly before a stroke deprived the good doctor
himself of speech.

Martha serene and radiant at eighty; and Lawrence in
the Brink Institute, they tell me he is exercising and learn-
ing to walk again. And what's-her-name . . . you idiot, can't
recall the monosyllable of your old friend, you nameless
name dropper, lost all your pocketful of names. Ah, yes—
Ruth—she's back by name! Her postcard came, lively as
ever, from her house in Poverty Hollow, in the hardest

winter we can remember; she's not flying South; and when I saw her last I noticed among the papers on her work table (sneaky peeker that I am) a donor application blank from an eye bank.

> My friend Bogie the poet
> who was stabbed to death on Second Avenue,
> he too, once long ago
> haunted a gray news sheet,
> his scarecrow trick-or-treat
> out on the street by early morning:
> the hollows of his ravaged face in idle dusk,
> the spidery wrist and webbed ethereal hand of age.

5

With a sigh and a prayer I settled on the couch as my breath at last slowed from the exertion of arrival. The door flew open and Sylvia dashed in and made off with the telephone book. Shocked out of my morning's laborious climb and knocked downhill again, with a rip in my hernia, which was sewed up only a year ago by Dr. Lazarus.

What rage in her leaping eye and flying hair, turning in tearful fury as she pulled the door after her and left it ajar as usual.

"Close the door!" I screeched in agony, "please, please!" A vengeful slam of the door, for somehow she has no talent for closing doors and it falls to my lot to close them after her; and then I start my climb back to my morning's labor, yet once more oh ye laurels, and must I back on my feet and to the door again? and three turns in my lair and bed myself down for my journey into space.

In a flash our gray striped tigercat Tommy streaks across the room in unbelievable leaps from corner to corner to table-top to the highest bookshelf and back to my couch to wriggle into his privileged place under my writing board for a sleep as long as my pen continues to scratch away.

This you see is our ever burning predicament, our entrapment in a snarl of woes; like those in the daily comic strips and in the joke books carried about by hobos in their jeans, and displayed on the corner newsstand. It was just another warning instant, a premonition rising from the darkness of the gypsie dream book on the magazine rack next to the joke book, of the moment about to crash over our heads and reveal man's fate.

From my horizontal point of view whatever I see that stirs and figures in the present appears only in this aspect of suspense, in anticipation of the moment to come, like a ship whose constant rise and fall reiterates its condition of being, that of ever hanging on the next roll of the tide which for all we know may swell into a flood to swallow the Empire State Building.

What a fool to go on taking risks, at a time like this! A shiver and a little stab in the chest, having been spared so long, at ease and going great, to say goodbye before my time! A fair wind for France, only to drop the boom and knock the wind out of me. Why, when I might have gone abroad forty years ago with that dear clown Hirsch, when everybody went and changed the world and I stayed home. And now in my last chance, last breath, certain little warning signs; the weather has changed and the wind is northeast from the sea, and a pang in my side tells me I too have altered, in my grammetry, as I mimic the world, harmoniously seismic with the cosmic and a stormy incoming tide. And the weather man with his isobars and fronts, with the clockwise highs and cyclic lows, and his planetary photo transmitted by telestar, offers another trivial variant of the same windy old story from space.

•

Anywhere, said Sylvia, so long as we went and so long as she need not serve dinner and were served instead; and I told her I had looked all over the map and couldn't find a place called Anywhere. She wanted me to act out the ritual of choosing the place she had already set her heart on; a little argument that started back in 1918, when Emanuel had remarked with a short laugh that she was *slowly* driving me mad.

I feel a little feverishness coming on in my bones, a melting half-sweet dizziness as of hemlock; how can I be so foolhardy, to risk flying South?

> Having rolled my stone all the way up this hill,
> to let go once again, and fly away,
> fly away mirth, and back to earth and die
> on some barbarous shore like Miami Beach.

Like my escape from this Minotaur island when I broke out of the bull pen on Madison Avenue, where a radio was roaring a ballad about a hurricane, carrying on about a youth overboard and a drowning. Of my sea journey I remember only how I won the broad jump, competing with a black lad rescued from a wave-battered skiff named *Narcissus*. On the moldy steerage deck of the old steamer ripping ahead southward with dolphins bounding at the bows, I took my turn in the contest with the Polack, the Chinaman, the Black and a Spanish teacher on a trip to Yucatan. As I made my winning jump and landed near the deck rail, my big silver watch flew from my vest pocket in a high leap out to sea, trailing its flashing chain like a comet. It came to rest at sea bottom, ticking away somewhere between the Florida coast and Havana harbor. It was not I, just my timepiece, that went overboard, for I sailed on to port and back alive. One day at last I stood again on the planks of the long Hudson dock with my suitcase and subway fare home to Sylvia.

I knew I wouldn't dare leave home again for a nightmare voyage aboard a ship rushing on yet making no headway, laboring toward an ever retreating, ever more distant shoreline. But when Sylvia with darkened face passed me in the hall my heart turned over. I remembered how once in the middle of a quarrel I surprised her with such a prankish yielding to her wish that she broke down and cried. So that night as she sat at a game of solitaire, deftly turning up a card for slow appraisal, I thought I'd try again.

"Listen, dear," I said, "I wouldn't mind going to Miami Beach." Total absorption in the turned-up card. "It's what you want, isn't it? So let's go South? Away from arthritis and migraine, just pack and go! I'd work an hour a day, no more. Where the birds have flown?" Then I said bitterly: "That's twice I've asked you." She laid down another card and studied it. Unbroken silence.

She had been crying. She had not told me that she had been to the eye doctor. And now the familiar word for it escapes me, plays hide and seek with me and blanks out in the psychiantics of the tricky mind, a tiny little insomniac antibody that has fled out of sight. I despair of those three little vanished syllables . . . *aha!* what a word for it . . . *cataract!* On her chart the doctor had written: *nuclear sclerosis, both eyes.*

So here I am again, on the subway platform, once more underground, in the dismal tunnel with its leaking walls and rotting railbed, in the flickering netherworld of my recurring dream. On my way to my nephew Robert in his laboratory in the Burke Memorial Building to pick up the package for Sylvia and meanwhile get his advice on the most eminent eye man.

I climbed the stair to daylight and crossed the frozen square toward the cliffs of the great hospital complex. Past the marble entrance hall and onward to the fifteenth floor.

Lost again, in a tiled corridor running westward, narrowing to a faraway turn.

In his private office at last, by the high window on the New Jersey skyline, I found Robert seated cozily at his desk, smiling up through an idea, three sharp little creases on his shining brow above the glint of his glasses. We went on a brief tour of his laboratory. He leaned an arm on the edge of a huge dial-studded cabinet and said: "You must have seen one of these in your friend Christopher's lab." "All I remember," I said, "is him standing and shaking a bottle of heavy water and letting me take it and shake it." "So actually," he smiled, "you had a hand in the history of science."

I got home with Sylvia's package and helped her unwrap the new mink jacket and try it on.

"I thought it would cheer me up," she said, turning in front of the hallway mirror, "and now that I have it, it doesn't make any difference."

It was the evening of the concert at Lincoln Center. There, as though by a miraculous escape we would return to our places up above in the azure twilight of our top balcony seats, the last among the highest. We would be early, the orchestra would still be out, their chairs still empty, and not a string would tremble until they filed back on stage; and not a hint of the world that would come to pass—for you cannot read music, you heretic of hearsay and passing sound, lucky you are not hard of hearing. By the miracle of so few who made music, what have you but your rumors and snatches of the far-off City of Sound, of the lore of man's incessant heart, beating time, year by year, in your hungry, humming little trumpet shell, in your empty ignorant cold forgetful ear?

6

Just what is it that's going on, and what goings on!—a little nothing, singly piping out in glee, aglow in a three-note echo and refrain and again and again in my hearing and knowing, and rightly now I could explain, and might have lost it all! and knew it all along, like that dear hippie goof on TV, confiding and confused, you know, hung up on a phrase, you know, a brave shy bird cry on the wing; explain this if you can, and to whom, and in the words of what realm and time? for you're in it, in a sense, deep in a present or a past, where you needed your sleep and slept your way through and woke up, a waker!—a guest with glass in hand, a bourbon on the rocks; dreaming you had arrived in the new world for another round of worldly seeking and striving, riding off from the parking lot with Sylvia in your old '51 Plymouth.

As happily as Amadeus the darling child with flushed cheeks and dancing eyes obeys when his venerable companion stoops down with a kiss and a command: "Now run along and play!" and he dashes to the piano and the new little tune starts with a tinkle, and you turn around and it's the Piano Concerto at Lincoln Center.

So don't panic, all the world listening, by arrangement with the Society of J. Joyce Jehova, present at an event, a concatenation, at what has become of us, so comely so becoming, something wonderfully lovely of you, so glad you could come! and as you see we arrived! at a play, a party, a gathering, for that was all there was to it: to show, to appear, to be, to be awake! The truth, old Finney, is simply in waking up as you did at dawn when the sun "pranced in like a bridegroom," a consummate player; and as I opened my eyes by no act of intention or volition and by no fault of my own, when all's well awake and whole in a glance just as I come to myself on a frosty morning, born again to heaven and earth.

Like little padre Casals on Channel 13, baggy and
stringy, loosely tied together, as he firms his jaw a bit awry
and glares into your soul; and a nod and a tap on wood, to
start again, master and pupil one, and instant by instant,
by the wisp of the instant, by the beating atom of time,
by the breathing strings, once more the evocation of the
slow rising Oh, like the lute of Israfel whose speech is song.
Fearless and shameless, like rainbow and halo, the cello
voice of a tiny little distant man; and they adored him, he
too exiled overseas by the horned beast that snores in Spain.
Pablo, for whom companions reached to help him from the
podium, and bore him down the aisle and home on his
spindle legs to his study and his couch and a short nap.

> His bow rounds a slow arch in the air,
> his growl, vibrato, swells and fades,
> urgent, tender: "like a rainbow?"
> (gnarled and mellowed ninety years
> and hardly bigger than his cello):
> "arching like a rainbow, yes?"
>
> Lightning in the master's eye!
> Falter, and heaven is undone,
> or wake and rise on the wing
> with the throbbing rainbow Oh!
> for he with cello voice is blessed,
> playful darling of the world,
> and he is worldliest and best.

Once every mother dreamed her little girl would play
the piano and the boy would practise violin and everybody
in the world would read music and listen like the little
white dog with ear cocked at the cornucopia horn in the
old Victrola trade mark; and everybody would grow up a
member of the orchestrahaha, to play Beethoven and sing in
the Messiah Chorus. And all join the communist Christian
Church and do as Jesus said, follow me and leave father

and mother and abandon hope all ye marihuanians and sit and stare into the sun.

"Casals is a dear man," said my friend Anton, "but that is quite beside the question of his music; the way he plays Bach, that interminable drag of the passionate bow . . . . draarraaah . . . . drives me up the wall!"

7

My nephew Tom's small hands suggest the light touch and the soft tread. Within that softness sleeps a lion, at whose sudden roar I once saw three-year-old Jamie darken and swell with instant bruising all over as the tears appeared.

> Little Jamie on his knees
> runs his bright red toy across the carpet,
> making dreamy sounds of a mighty truck
>
> Which gigantically arrives
> raging down Tenth Avenue!
>
> The husky boy at the wheel
> is deaf to his wake of havoc,
> venting in the world's face,
> his rearward plume rising to join
> a gathering false dusk
> to appal the pilots in the sky.

Tom speaks only when prodded into a smiling quip or raised eyebrow, and slips right back into the subculture where he has his being. His is the bright-browed head with the small rococo features, the dancing eye, the poise of the well endowed, who had never known want or wound, or so seemed to one who was deprived and warped with envy.

Tom sent his friend Charles up to see me. From an

impulse to be charitable, to dig him, to be with it, whatever
the big new dream of transgressing youth, I went along
with his plea for help in launching his holiday art show.

> A tough young dandy in jeans and sandals
> his face ringed by a beard of antique trim
> comes round and turns up at my pent house door
> as pretty as a Christmas minstrel
> and ruins my day, old uncle that I am.

Charlie's face smiling up from the open portfolio is
guileful and flushed with mischief. Encouraged, it grows
self conscious and almost confessional; he is surprisingly
like old Alex, charmer of a prior age who is now a whole
year dead. And I have seen that same tentative look of
daring lurking in my niece Fanny's clever eyes.

Deluded, chesty, high-shouldering, forward vaulting
youth! And yet, at sight of the face eager and dissembling,
suffused with the wilful, unaware beauty of the passionate
child, my knowing heart is touched with a parental pang.

Charlie could not suspect that it was his luck to be medi-
ocre. A mere hint of it might bring on an uneasy fatigue
and a low grade fever. The help of an old ex-adman like
me was really nothing and I let him bask in approval and
make a great bid for praise. I might have turned him down
if I were not still drugged by the fumes of my past on Mad
Avenue; like having another bad dream of still doing a
piece for a client, as when Randy White showed up in a
sweat about just one last art work deadline, and how could
I say no? And there was Fred Bamberg, deep in his termi-
nal folly, in ever-scheming limbo, the old demon fallen
to such straits; for a whole Sunday late into the evening
reading his indomitable pentameters into my tape recorder
and then forgetting to take home the precious tape.

Such charity to a virtual stranger, and yet I have still to
send a word of condolence to my cousin Sadie whose hus-
band died more than a month ago. Last year on a visit East

she had said with a wry nod and the black humor which is the gift of the chosen, those who are marked for irreparable misfortune: "So it had to be me, to be blessed with a colostomy!" and wept when she learned that I in fact was one of them; that in the same year just past I too had been made "a member of the Club."

The things that catch my eye! smoke gets in my eye, and how many strikes in the eye, a black eye for blue-eyed you, for black is my favorite color. The item in a back page of the *Times,* a short piece about ten youths high on LSD who sat in a row and stared at the sun until their sight was quite burned out, painless in heaven; heliotropic flower children, they had turned to cosmic Light, staring stone blind, with amulets and jingle bells of perpetual Christmas, with Buddha, Donne and Blake, for they were, like, well donne to a crisp, blaked in deed as in word, in disenchantment with the elders; as a sign of faith in Love, a talisman for mankind, at the farthest Western shore, nearest the Orient across the Sea of Peace, my heart in San Francisco, on a trip, a trip, alas, doomed by the fault of a four letter word like Love to walk in night the rest of their lives, with a stick and a dog's eye to guide from curb to curb, to reach out a hand like a black ant's feeler all night long.

Eager to be welcomed, with an urgency near desperation; in a baffling slang from the streets of East Village, pleading with a colossal monolitho close-up of the teletone moonface of Dean Rusk. Inspired youth, lavish in passion, wasting its outrage in appeals to a pre-recorded answering service.

> For the love of godliness in the season of goodness,
> what's the dear world coming to,
> oh Jesus on a short visit?

What a drag, the turn of the year, and I a child of the century, age seventy. Still time to settle our account and pay off and get by, not too far in arrears, with the threat of penalties and atonement. How come, with the first of the month, programmed to self-search, we duly awake to report, to file and to deposit! Ezra the devaluated Pound had a system for that, hung up on usury and a phobic panacea for the world's ills. And there was Schillinger, the nervous little man who wolfed his dinner one evening in our apartment, who played Bach backwards and taught art at Columbia as a special case of the binomial theorem, and incredibly was teaching George Gershwin his mathematical theory of composition. And Rovy the aged piano teacher was ever ready with an anecdote about him, told with a fierce malicious smile.

But more appalling was the literary magazine I discovered in a bookshop window, the entire issue devoted to an anthology of Computer Poetry. Alarmed, I hurried to my room to write a reply to the insolence of the computer.

And there was general disbelief that World War Three had already begun. Forget it and please don't be your insistent old self; oh, come on! and settle for a creeping nemesis, with an anæsthetic whiff of faith though there is no faith, war but should we not declare it? Reminded me of an old-hat poet who was famous in New York speakeasies during World War One. It was Donald Evans, who proposed in his Preface to *Sonnets From The Patagonian* that a battalion of sonneteers march on Berlin armed with silk hats and silver-tipped walking sticks.

Again, despite all, something inconceivable, devised to confound you and trip you up, a mysterious perversity, a counter-intelligence appears and contradicts you.

Around a great circular table ceremonious men are exchanging ponderous insults; a performance that started with a little opening play on a bridge deck on the dancing waves of the Pacific, on the other side of the laughing face of the world. Broadcast live in daylight by satellite radar, playing a dangerous game of hide and seek, like the game of search and destroy, where the dawn comes up across the bay, the same old game, though by a change of rôle and by another set of players; and you see that all are in it, to aid a progress or dance attendance or stand by, who also serve, in the pay of the CIA, each naturally sending and receiving in code, awaiting and making his play, sworn orders in strange attire, in hood or gown or tails and black tie. In a ship's cabin, from a finger on a key tapping out its tune to the air waves, as quick as the merry eye and flushed cheek of little Amadeus, as sudden as the tinkle of the piano tune, the word leaps round the world, news of a new move in the game, and calls the world to the round table at the UN for the next play in the gambit of the cloak and dagger gamboliers in a very old ritual script, to deal with a mechanical dove shot down over Russia.

In the close-up on the TV screen a simple thing of word by word and name by name and face to face at a gathering of events to a showdown, a happening that was to be despite all and however we turn and return about and foul play.

8

A full page ad in the New York Times, HOSTAGES FOR PEACE, proposed to take the problem away from the Kremlenins and the Pentagonists and start a massive civilian exchange program to make sure there were too many of us there and too many of them here for a mutual blow-up, no joking matter; another numbskull fantasy, but can you do better, can you stop the clock ticking you away from here? Can't you even rage like my friend Emanuel? Beat that clock and call all those dear family men in there at their closed circuits and their underground moon maps, and kick over their drawing boards and swivel chairs.

Did you see the stony old Presidential face, how tired it was, as he read from the invisible teleprompter? The glitter of his glasses almost hid the unrelenting old eyes; such pallor, such weariness, a mask where anguish lurked, like the shudder in the yiddish phrase from hell: *zu lachen mit yashcherkis,* to laugh with hilarity induced by the sting of scorpions. The TV screen is said to make men transparent. This old man has but a short span to edit his papers for a memorial archive, yet he wants another term in the White House and expects to run, tired heart and all; and an armistice will win it for him and the war will resume in due course, the earth is theirs to split to open wide to enter and join the dinosaurs.

The news flash from the Far East, a shot in the camera eye, turned me into a shadow. The gunman in the field told the newsman with the mike: "That roaring sound is the flies. They drown out the jets." Heard round the world, shivered the uncomprehending sphere, drilled the dazed mind, seized you by the hair.

There goes the door buzzer, from way down below on street level, it can't fly so high, haha, they must have got wind of what's going on up here, going about our business: telling the posthumous world what they did out there. The newsreel flicker quickens to a stop and over. Like the lightning stroke and open grave in the rain; like a TV flashback to World War Two, to that other Judgment Day of a blast and a silence. Time stood still for just a minute for the world to see what was and had been.

And here in the rising storm of city sound rattling my window, it was my intention to make just that one point to suffice me for the day, and sustain me over the roaring; a mere point, a premise for the whole cockeyed euclidean sphere.

It is rumored that the Mafia, and a Texas oil tycoon, a small bald anticoon, an anticommie cracker with a senile head tremor, have been buying up and merging book publishers and putting them on the stock market tickertape, and the textbook companies will getty little children into telephone booth cubicles with pushbutton learning machines.

A little demonstration in circularity, how I got around to sending the coupon to the National Committee Against The Crime of Silence. In response I received a little button to wear in my lapel, a copy of the Declaration I had signed, and a small card for my wallet. Recorded and numbered among the comically vulnerable, the exposed and doomed: you see what was manifest there. To stand up to be marked and counted once again and once for all under history's yellow star; it was something after all was it not, to mail that Declaration.

Was it daring of me? Or was it timid, soft voiced, inoffensive, clearing the throat and cooing, a dove, a winged, angelic white American? Long aware of secret preparations for detention centers; and yesterday's sight of the troops dragging gassed youths by their heels across the paved square of the nation's shrine of law and order, in the capital of the Free World.

Shades of Robert Lowell! Shades of Aunt Amy and her cigar, in her heavy serge suit, bemused in her patterned garden! Gentle, melancholy, wry Robert, as sad as the fate of kings, who sat in the TV studio cross-legged, hands clasped on knee, the unspoiled scholar's smile on his upturned face, a strong young father's face, as he sat listening to the brash big-fisted Russian youth declaiming verses from the land of Pushkin and Prince Mishkin and Yevtushenko.

Shades of Skid Row, of time lost as a night worker, and many a wakeful night on my back on the sand, gazing up at the stars from a rock-bound beach, where the crescendos of the dirging surf were my lullabyes.

Shades of my freezing youth in that outside time of zero weather. The locked door, the drawn blind, the blank stare, the closed for the day and gone for the night and not at home and moved away and no address and do not enter; stopped cold in the subway by a turnstile with a coin slot.

Chilled in a sudden vision of the bone and claw of the sons of the Bald Eagle, shooting craps and cap pistols for the rights of man and pipe lines and tidelands; of a mob in the electric night of Times Square ebbing to and fro through the side streets like the millrace from the tide; and in the crossfire of spotlight beams the giant wall poster of the idol with the blue pouched jowls and cosmetic smile and the predatory squint of imperial prophecy; at his side a four star aide checking the score of the Allied dead.

And on the newsstand rack, the husk of the face of Dean Rusk and the counter-face of his Russky counterpart, icy Siberian Kosygin at the U.N., jointly reading a draft resolution censuring Israel.

Shades of trim little Jimmy Devan at his files and his adding machine, his old eyes recessed in a cobweb of wrinkles, who as a youth flew a plane in World War One. He is now more haggard than ever and quicker to anger. His grandson in the parochial school filling in his picture coloring book with crayon smears over outlines of Jesus, a bleeding heart, a crown of thorns, and martyrs with glazed eyes, flayed alive or impaled with spikes and burning arrows.

And priestly affable Bernie Cohane in black serge who sold advertising space in *The Parish Monthly Letter* and once in confidence denounced me to the executive V.P. as a commie atheist.

And Jerry White whose short left arm snatched the commission on one of my accounts when I was laid up at home with the flu. He was from an orphanage school of hard knocks where by uncounted clouts about the head and the sting of the spare rod he had been tempered to the fellowship of the fast buck and the nixonian chuckle. A short life misspent in disfiguring and defacing and fouling up the past. The unalterable past, region of the ill favored, unvoiced, undone, denied, dissolved and atomized, seed of catastrophe.

9

Locked in by a cold spell, I haven't been out since last night when I was driven off the ice-sheathed sidewalk into the traffic stream by swift staggering blows of the wind. By a gust of sheer luck I tacked back to the curb and slid all the way home to my mountainous hot-house tower of blazing windows. It glowed in visionary space among the stars, a total brooding presence, by height and distance transmuted into a golden luminescence in the blue-black darkness, insubstantial, abstract and astronomical. Seen and believed, beheld and contained, though the grandeur melt in solar wind, though it smoke away in space, in sign by sign in the sky. Mark by mark, relic by relic, with the image, the ballad, the hymn, the tear, the dream and the graffiti on the subway wall. Symbol by symbol; in a ballistic sense [*sym,* together; *bol,* throw] a good show. What a gathering, what a dispersal!

A drill gang from a Con Edison truck has torn open the pavement exposing a yawn of raw earth and an intestinal tangle of cable and steam pipe. The power drill clamor of excavation leaps all the way to the sonic slam of a passing jetliner. Siren wails flee over Eighth Avenue, dying in the northward traffic. The snow, dazzling white on the rooftops, is already fouled in the streets. A smokestack rising from a thirty-story pile of grimy granite is pouring up a small black mushroom cloud.

All that is audible here has a driving, pounding insistence impossible to fathom. As I listen, it wakens a silent, prophetic image in my past. There I stand in an empty store I had rented in a condemned building on the East Side. The door had warped and fused with the frame, the lock would not turn; the waterless sink in the rear, the twist of lead pipe from the denuded wall—and even the window glass—were singed with ash and scummed with a dungeon phlegm.

I lost a night's sleep down there in the Blackout. It was after closing time when the fuses blew. I was alone in my office on the seventeenth floor. I felt my way in the dark along the hallway wall, past the dead elevators and through the fire exit and groped down the steel stairwell in helical descent. My last match blistered my thumb as I reached the street level and came out through the lobby into the frozen night swept by headlight beams and lashing turret beacons and a pandemonium of braying horns. The fire trucks, their motors running, seemed to be waiting for word from some high command to move, to breach the canyon glut of stalled cars. I went for shelter to the Bank Street entrance of the Westside Savings Bank, a client of mine. I rang the night bell, which responded faintly in the deep interior, and at last the guard came, blinding me with his flashlight, and led me through a side door, bypassing the giant iron grille to the banking floor, where I dozed and groaned in a straight chair until dawn. Then I set out on foot on the journey north toward home, and so ended another rehearsal of Doomsday.

All were journeys back it seems to me. I've been around, and always back to the States, and back to bed, and back to daytime. On a rotting boat from Yucatan, through a hurricane, where young Crane had jumped from the deck. Once north across the border, sailing on Lake George, pursued by death from a snake bite, and back alive by train; I've been around.

And down in dark-alley Chicago, when bohemian tea rooms had other names, and none so forlorn as I; how I came and how I got out, search me! In the murk of that candle-lit joint I actually heard the two lesbians who owned the place arguing about me. They were in the next booth, their hushed voices almost drowned in the crush and clatter of the dinner hour. Somebody in there was defending poor devil me; a matter of non-payment for the soup and hard seeded rolls I had eaten there every evening that week. The short one in mannish tweed was being brutally blunt, and her soft-spoken partner was vague and plaintive. When they came over to my table for the showdown, I remember smiling and frowning as I offered to work it off if they would hire me as one of those sandwich men who march about wearing an advertising sign. It was one of the things I almost was for a time out there, before I got out and got away. Like when I was booked for a bout with a Cuban lightweight in Merida for a prize of seventy five dollars, to pay my hotel bill; but there too, *almost;* and trained for it a number of days before I got away and back to the States.

On my unwilling legs to the tiny patch of park on Ninth Avenue to sit with the old survivors. I brought along a pad and pencil, and a derelict woke up and eyed me. Happily awhile the easy breath and sweet amnesia in the light of day; the night world well lost; what's with me? no one ever knows, a blessing after all, though in the terminal decade the deadline is in sight; it is like the pre-dawn look in the mirror, when the internal alarm goes off: *time, mister!* and the heart contracts, how can one bear to leave the long year's scribble in such disarray?

Alone with my art in my ark, my biblical self afloat in my storm of being, foundered aground, stranded by loss of a word; to lose the world for want of a little fallen dove; come now, sing it back into being, near and dear, awake and alight and alive.

Again the rattle-rat upstairs, I'll erase him from my final hour if it kills me! I'll let myself out into the city air pouring up and away like a conflagration, where I weather in the wind; for this is what I do, I beat about, to rise to the event of flight, of soaring to presence, in the blaze and shade, in the messiah sun's millenium.

And then, where was it, short of breath, with what eloquence I launched on my scheme to start a one-man magazine, maybe like Edgar Allan Poe x-ing a paragraph and tarred and feathered in the end. I had a name for it and a diabolical strategy for financial support, which I expounded to Zabel Silbur the sculptor, his hands up over his ears, his head bent, with a despairing smile pleading: *"Please, Moe, no more, excuse me, my head!"* for he was convalescing from a head injury in a car smash-up.

And of all the near things the nearest, dare I tell it?— was that early Sunday morning when the lightning struck me in the groin, in that region of the world which was me, which was old and human.

Of That Region

Outside my window, tremors of the new day
like dancing gnats in the cold sun,
fevered with the unborn Spring.

I was with the fallen lost to sight.
With doomsday bell and yammering siren,
airless and fever swelled, I ballooned to the moon
and wept in space.

Racing the nightmare cloud,
in the deathward ward, the curtain drawn
between me and a dying man,
sobbing in unison
as the beat of his agony played me,
plucked cry by cry my high-strung frame.

In that place, in that plight,
I wake or dream a seeking face

nearing and peering into mine
as I nod and pass away
and ride a mile
of tunnel walled in white immortal tile,
to a stop at X-ray.

There I lay turning colder
in my bleached laundered shift
open at the rear
for probing access to my hidden realm.
waiting, among the passing,
for the white masked angels and ministers
of the grace and the pityfogging ways
of particular being.

All undergone
and by the luck of the weak and the meek
rescued and lifted back
to hear the miracle of my return
from unknown to unknown,
to lie in state and grant an audience
to the chastened, the believers.

Visiting hours over, must go now,
make my getaway while I may
for it hurts to stay, and the rates
are high per diem.

A wisp of the absent truth:
that I wanted away, a waif,
a mere wishbone of my former self,
where I lay outside the world.

All as freakish to me
as the visiting patriarch
of the Byzantine Church,
a father of fathers, gricky and tricky,

with the lordliest, shaggiest beard and brow,
more prickly, more sickly by far
than micky dicky me, so spare me
that ancient seminary cant
and bear with me, and do not cry.

From my bed of abstinence I know you,
darling reader my good physician with lively eye
scanning my film,
my martyred, light pierced phantom,
my visible mere me,
by a mysterious charity, silent from the sublime,
where I had been astounded by loss of breath,
to find my way home, and cling and fail.

Ratman

The old ratman's back, a gentle-seeming
ghoul of hell in our time,
and taps away like a fanatic pulse,
as faint, intent,
as mouse or louse of ancient plague,
to claw and cling and nest
in the fine rot crawl of old city wall,
to invade me in my sleep,
enter my tender fold and gnaw my bone
(and show up on my X-ray)
thief of my mind and my sound,
to end the world and none to weep.

Ratman lets drop a grain of gall,
it rolls into a nail-hole in the floor.

Three quick taps
for ways that are dark and peculiar,
to rap me out, to tap my time away,
and I'll crack him, black him, snap his line,
is what I naught to do. I'll call him:
One more tap from you
and up and beat your brains out.
I'll say it quick and quiet,
he'll sweat, and will he dare
pick up his little hammer
and tap out a leer of defiance, would I should I
break in his door, or eat myself up in defeat
under my ceiling under his floor?

That is the secret of it all,
that he is above me and over my head
in this tapping order of the old pecking order
of the old order, as the slumlord said
on his TV appearance from behind the law,
lord of the lowly.

It was nothing at all, that little thunderclap!
from way out in the world once more
a power-drill rattled, zoomed,
a chopper in the air spun by,
flopped by my window jumpy as a bat;
stampeding up Eighth Avenue the freightcar trucks
blew their sooty gas and gnashed their brakes.

It's almost noon, too loud, too near,
dear me, a deathening of the ear.

Surprise him like a tiger at the door.
Pow! Zing! and leave no clue,
skip to my lair and lie low.
Silence that upstairs borer,
his gravel head and earthworm lip,

his snaggle fang and cyclops eye,
hovering, gasflame in the eye.

Ping! in the eye, dropped dead,
and down the stair, my heart still gulping air,
all the way home to my room and have a look,
and cop out, opt out, stop the bombing,
pull out by helicopt,
out of vietkingkong hungho dingdong,
back to silence and world peace.

Is this the way to run a world?
cowardly brave! chief white feather dove!
me down to my dive and die, sleep with my fathers,
pray to Great White Father
of promises, good lore and ordure,
who changed me into small change,
who stained my name and soiled the truth,
swore out a warrant,
fouled the record and the deed
in the safe in Town Hall.

Alienative, alienerican Red,
back in Black tribe
where I belong ago with Hiawatha, feather-head,
and smell like whisky warrior,
dead as a mackerel in Bowlder Dam
in silt of fake white man lake,
lost again, too late, no luck with fate,
sick of my past, present, pfut! no light no heat,
just one fuse blow the whole Atlantic coast,
one flash from North to South to instant peace,
blind by what power by what now?

Return

Once more, by death's dirty trick,
on the starlit highway.
By headlight by flashlight to this same
same, same
infernal crossing,
my locus pocus focus
my attitudes and latitudes
my cunning old brain
my ragged roadmap, failed me,
failed me,
curling away, parting at the folds.

A Near Thing

On my polar night journey to dawn,
I sighted no white bear, no whaler's mast,
but by a wolfish slip of fate,
by the span of a walrus tusk, a near thing,
awoke to this.

In the fragile pane, peering through frost,
eye to eye, in panic wonder,
despairing sight outfacing me,
my opposite number, escaped from sleep
to nowhere in a glass,
to sigh like this,
to seek and see, to flee and barely be,
and touch a secret charm
in breast or pocket.

By the strange arrangement of the sea,

and machination of the mind,
my nonsense in the dark stared back,
a swimming eye.

(I was ripping along full sail,
dashing along,
when this happened to me.)

The Doorbell

The doorbell tinkle toll, and little Jamie
ringing in the living room,
Oh, keep them I pray, dear Sylvia, from my door.
A voice rasps through the plaster wall,
fulfilling the Messiah's promise
of universal dissemination
by theogenital descent, by Our Father
who so loved, like Leda's swan.

Sylvia at the door, Jamie and his toy behind her,
Out! Out! and how she glared, I was incinerated.
One more shout and they are out,
you chooser, you refuser, and now where are you,
you wary nary scary loser,
out of the corner where I arararar, where I are no more
in my puff of air.

Passed away in the Christmastide, wished away,
washed down in the tidings of the bloody lamb
on Christmas morning.

Were you there, have you known
sundering, undergoing, red sea passage
fleeing the hosts and the odds?

And the devil to pay in the living room
on my day of atonement
for my cruelty to little Jamie, my shout
to bar them out.

Jingle jangle the bell, and Jamie-mouse squeaking
as grandma comes and carries him off,
and I unseemly in the bathroom,
startled by a stain like Christmas crimson,
on a Holy Day; spare them, Father,
keep them painless and abstract sweet
and safe in Latin.

This, however, being where I dwell
and what I am and how I fare
on my solemn enterprise,
launched early in the morning
upon the leaping surf,
come hell and high water

Here I am, my fancy,
to carry on and be carried away,
I made my bed the sea.

Can't Sit Here

My door shut, my bed as narrow
as in my gaslit youth
in a dark green hall.

Oh, one could weep
to find oneself in just this twist of the past!
wake up, you loon, you echoing whippoorwill

In the descending dark,
skimming the meadow hollow,
loud in the orchard trees,
are you a small bird? swinging high
swinging low
in the dark ward of sleep.

The doorbell rings
and there stands a small black angel
glowing large-eyed, with full red lips,
bringing my Christmas cards from the press,
so all's not lost,
very likely a lot of *merde,*
a word I prefer to the English
for I am a timid man
and evasion is my *forte,*
never to confront, never declare,
no, not at crazy odds like these!

Have I called on old Ben since his stroke?
last of the items marked *Urgent*
scattered all over my desk,
memos loose in the air
flying about like pet pigeons.

Side by side with folded wing
they roost on the maple bough
above the park bench chalked all over
with leprous droppings
(can't sit here).

A Crazy Script

And this was not my wish or plan,
to be speeding in my Plymouth
for the rockbound Jersey shore
with Sylvia at my side
and a pang in my breast, here we go again,
just when I thought, all's well in my heaven
in the fresh country air
and now this! a crazy script, right in the midst
of history and letters, coughing in the cold.

In the eve of my life, back on Mad Avenue,
woe betide me, back at my trade
at worse than death in a silk hat,
in an office with a client, laying out an ad
for their pen with that name of strange device,
the mightier pen
for wordplay by airy nothings
by penmanship on anything anywhere
on walls on sea on air
tracing hairline lifelines
in the skies signed over to United,
the worldly line for all who yearn
for freedom and a good return,
where the deer and the antelope dally
and bells ding dong all day
for the dolls in death valley
and nobody calls my number,
none any no more.

Poet's Funeral

By the high Gothic door, from a huddle of mourners
young Richard in a dark flourish of beard
came up for a solemn handshake.

Oh, for a Virgilian guide
(pardon an old-hat megaloman's
immodest allusion)
through Amnesia and Aphasia
where still I live to tell,
having by the underground returned
to being in the world,
treading the very bounds
of tolerance and charity,
an idle caller at the door.

I knew him, a sweet old wretch
with shrunk cheek flushed and famished eye,
already nameless,
one more unfortunate, he passed away
in his own poor verses.
I heard him in a tavern once
recite a raffish doggerel on God,
like a smart cleric in the bosom of the church,
whose God could take a little levity;
for his taste was catholic
and he had been welcomed into the fold
amid the hushed whisperings of friends.

The funeral service was brief and uneasy,
the priest's recital seemed to hint
that all was not well with this agèd boy in the casket,
with arms crossed on breast like Thomas à Kempis,
in the tinctured gloom of this rich man's church,

the gentle roaring of the organ pipes,
the last look and the slow march
for an ex-yiddish pauper taken in and away
and off to nowhere.

Night Bird

Half awake, he sat on his rooming house bed
and answered me thus:
"Same as ever, working, drinking, screwing."
It is the irreversible truth
that this was what he said,
and how he spent his time, life, fortune
and sacred honor; and is no more,
lone wolf, provocateur and bounty hunter
with a bitchy short bark-laugh,
a hearstwhile sophist of the pseudo-left,
an ambidextrous card-carrying fellow
of the devant garde rear.

Though someone warned: "That guy is dangerous,"
I could not show discourtesy
even to bat-winged hunger,
since I, poor youth, still died with Adonais
and wept with Mishkin, mourned with toothless Max
and learned by heart his meditations
on rattlesnake and hornèd toad.

A lump in the groin laid him low,
that mocking night-bird vanished
south of the border, in Villa country,
to join a cloak and dagger comrade
with a hammer and sickle under his sweater,
for sudden vengeance by the long arm

of the law of the dark
to strike at a celestial mind.

I heard it from a friend of a friend
who boarded a train with old John Dewey,
riding south to seek out the truth
of the blow that drove the hammer-point
into a scholar exile's brain,
ending the Kremlin triad
of the haggle of history:
how he rushed to his dear one crying:
"See what they have done to me!"
and fell to the kitchen floor.

There is a text by the fallen leader
which bears an emblem on the title page,
so poor a printer's mark
that none would ever ask, who drew that sign?
no witness now, none but my word,
that I was there, that it was mine.

White Father

To Friend and Foe Alike! the young man cried,
on a frosty morning in worldly light,
hat at the heart,
the anthem blasting brassy in the wind.

At the young White Father's side,
the failing sage, snow-blinded by the gods,
(the black band not yet sewn upon the sleeve)
trembled amid affectionate smiles,
squinting at the fluttering page,
in the dazzle of the Promised Land.

And the god-like young man
was quick to learn and quick to die,
as the moment struck and turned him off,
the same as everywhere
in rice field, wooded hill and rattling sky.

In the season of greetings,
of silvery bells, and coins in the kitty
for the lucky ones in the gamble
for who wins over the losers.

Hoarse from the long campaign, he cried:
To Friend and Foe Alike! and in reply
a silly trigger snapped and cracked the air,
sly Hell's device slipped through,
and he bled at once to nothing,
he was lost to himself and to the world.

The Hollow Carol

Christmas chimes in time of war.
Our city tower soars and trembles.
From the East, tidings by telestar

Of a dazzled desert plain,
a swarm of devils in the sun,
shepherds of the sudden dead.

Two, through the storm of maddened flies,
seize and toss one fallen cold:
he flutters to his high new bed.

By Silent Night, from World War Two
the captured films unreel
cadavers colliding down a chute.

A hushed mill's stacks
raise Gorgon heads of smoking hair,
where none dared look.

The locks are sprung, the gates flung wide,
the dead come through and stand and stare,
and make a hollow sound, intone

A senseless air.

The Crossing

A mark, a sign
of what is man, and by how many watts
to light up the world,
a little minus moon, a dizzy dot and dash
and chalk squeak on the blackboard wall:
by such devices an untimely dawn
blinded Hiroshima.

By your goddamned ciphering,
from your yiddish kop, mamserel of the world,
little mouse from the hold and the grisly oven,
why don't you go back and burn,
oh, the names they called you, little ghetto jewel,
they blew you across the world
with their breath of calumny and fear of the stranger
and his crazy ways of praying, by a ruined wall
or in a rented store unlit and airless,
from your vain divining,
from burning and freezing and strictly from fasting
and hiding and running scared,
schlemazel of history.

A notorious yeshiva swinger,
yanked quite out of his element
by the idealescent wisp
of his little goatee,
shining airborne through heaven
with his white-gowned bride and a bouquet
of wildflower lilies,
soaring over the Steppes,
over Europe, over the Atlantic,
bearing the six-pointed star
of crossed twined triangles,
misfortune's monogram.

This little stradivarius boychick,
of all the world the one who made that thing,
who found that sound and traced that name,
that sign and script, that new cabbala,
by gleam and gasp and antic semantic leap,
by creation, by the balls, and won the world,
oh, what a head on his shoulders,
this shinbony hunger child,
oh, what hollow hilarity,
at what a victory, what witch's brew
of schwere wasser, sea of flame.

Gimel

Enough of wishful, dark-drawn, black-face gothics
and bloodied hemologic,
an end of little fathers in their shawls
in their stalls by the wailing walls
of infinite lament, rehearsing sorrow,
the nauseous tear, the dead sea salt,
shalom, poor golem of Gehenna!

Goyim of golden rule and witch's brew,
of crucible and crucifix,
of star and trinity and canticle,
Goth, Gaul, Gael, of sword and spear and mace,
mail, chain and fist of steel,
converts, all,
of a bearded little Yossel from the East.

Out, lamp in Guernica! out, Eastern island!
incinerated by a Christmas star,
sunlight to starlight in an atom's twinkle.

Alas for babes and men, the halt and blind,
the weight of sorrows of how many G's,
the same old Glyph, of Generations,
of God, of Gonad, and of Gravity,
and of the Grave.

Sign of a world design,
and back to my own intent,
my Caligari box and monkish cell,
my exile isle in the West.

A Dove

How you do go on,
good grief, a clear and present danger,
shame, blush, pinko! send you away!
so defer
to the Great White Father knows best,
being white and a mother,
for he is patient, strong, silent and slow in speech,
so lone, alast, in the hearts of his countrymen,
and who among the poor

should then be first?
so not so fast, you!
and quiet, or riot!

Where are the mothers, old Spock in jail,
hawks and doves in war games, what to do?

Bill and coo, wear black,
weep to your Senator,
carry a placard to the Pentagon.

Mildly the lady with wind-blown hair:
"Why the National Guard? Police battalions?
The Secretary won't receive us? won't appear?
Afraid of a scrawl on their wall, and
Virginia Woolf at the door?"

What to do, lost on Mad Avenue,
back where I started to dissent
in nineteen hundred and seventeen.

Press Room

At the printer's a huge man-mushroom
was growing wider and wider in his swivel chair
like a waxing moon; an old pejorator,
steeped in the euphoria of the fleshy litho
of a spread-bottom floozy
on the pitted wall calendar.
He was a burst of self,
of the ever-same manimal,
roused to assail the strange
and aimed point blank at
insufferable me.

Heaven-bent to dwell and harp upon the truth,
in a passion to beat me about the head
with the wrongs in the name of the rights
of Humania!

Whipped out the engraver's eye-piece
and snapped it to the fine-screen litho print
to prove by the protruding eye,
for all who stood about and saw and heard,
above the presses beating out the headlines,
the first cause and the grand design
of his boorish blaze at my expense,
(for would I not be billed in the monthly mail
for my thankless part in the scheme of things?)
as the presses pulsed and shook the walls
and the ink flowed and the sheets were kissed
by the talk of the town
traduced from night to light of day
in cold blood and black phototype.

Fire

Gift wrapped in a ribboned box the pregnant bomb
had travelled to the fullness of its time
and blew and came out in the Post Office Building:
something common and internal that flamed into sight,
infernal bright, hohoho, hello, on a Yuletide,
the right time to blow by night time.

A distant starry toyland, sparks and jingle bells,
tinkling catastrophe. From the ringing red engines
the prancing fire fighters drop like ants
and vanish in steam and spray.

Lights out, the blind glass mountain pierced by flame,

the traffic lanes divide, the gongs and sirens dying,
crimson beacons swipe our eyes, whip past,
a spotlight plays on arching water spouts,
a fire truck waits awry across Tenth Avenue,
its warning lights pulsing like fireflies.

The darkened walls pour stench, the newborn ashes
swarm toward us and descend, dead on our window sill.

Emanuel

Emanuel awoke in a blind backyard room
and washed at the iron sink,
cupped his hands under the faucet
flaked with a scrofula of nickel crust;
naked as a snake in jungle dark,
a gleaming youth, sharp-ribbed with hunger,
his large, symbolic head
bright-eyed
like a gold-leaf sun or moon.

In the chill of the dead of night,
walked from the Bowery to Harlem
and whispered the cosmic fault:
"No one sees me, no one wonders at me!"
and wrote it in his composition book
of pages faintly ruled in blue,
with cardboard covers that would curl and part
like the peeling tenement walls
burning slow, shedding their airy ash
to be rebreathed by all who come about
and go about and share that air.

Phone Call

A voice as big as a bull fiddle
sang joyful in my ear: *Hello Uncle Moe!*
It was Eddie Mondesire,
happy to find me after twenty years,
his children grown, two girls, two boys;
his friend and partner died five years ago
and I've lost his name.

The Spring Street roost is gone,
the rotting loft afloat in curling fog;
and that far cry on the numbed ear
over the cascades of city roaring,
was it me? Oh my amnesia, my chasm,
my deep of blank, my ghost America,
above those torrents it rang archaic,
it was my sound.
By what freak gift from the blue,
what sky-high chance of echoing recall,
it sang! it happened
to a one-time battered bloodied
hoodlum slumhead
guilty of all that was ever told
of the criminal young,
briefly mentioned in the yellow
Chicago Literary Times
as another candidate for oblivion.

It gave me such a turn to see
that youth in foggy dew who was myself,
who by the ways of death is gone
like that lost name, I know it like my own.

They were a trio: Eddie
and Teddy the great salesman

who wore a button in his ear,
and my Black Hope diamond . . .
Neville was his name!

Hello dark Neville, say *Uncle Moe!*
the way Eddie said it on the phone.
You died of a doomed kidney,
my greeting card came back unread,
and I mourn you five years late.

Hello, inaudible whisper
which the ancients called soul,
in their idolatry of mark and sign,
(dread synonym of breath
by fearsome etymology)
you were the fiery one, the meteorite,
our Icarus, quenched in radiant day.

"It broke me up," said Eddie, "we were so close,"
and laughed, "none of us is getting any younger!
Crazy! this going off, and no way
to dial his number and turn him on,
and I go round and round this thing:
this being, and being gone."

Dear Young Guest

The youth's hair may be thick and rank
or saintly, matted like thorny hay,
or like the curls of the swordsman dandy
with his starched lace and steely wit,
or an unbrushed, pale and sorry lout
with belted leather and italian boot,
and a fever's bruise about the eyes.

An earthling, a strolling player
appears on stage,
on the steps of the Pentagon,
at the arch of the catacomb
of a prankish fraternity
forsworn to win the world
for the man in the moon.

An angel in San Francisco, a foundling waif,
the child's mysterious bloom
nesting in a foul tenement,
a sister lost, a brother in the news flash,
ah, dear young guest,
the world will light the Christmas tree
and take you to dinner in jail
in a Black Maria.

Before your time,
a dainty squeamish saint shipped off
to Nirvanah, whisky and tea
in a British counting house and garden,
and there was a gaunt and fiery one
who came to the Arizona sun
where first the Mushroom loomed,
flower of the West, Oh flower children,
where he coughed to death
among the furies of the leaping pulse
in a coal-faced miner's dream.

Another left home in the dark,
dragging his body's plight to such a death,
on a night highway
to the moon of no return.

And now the questioner who can't reply
hands you a lone star flower, the Iris,
the sigh of Osiris, the long "Alas!"

can't play it on your guitar, it won't rhyme.

Out of breath with all in flight,
castaway, exile founderer
snatched from the surf,
Enigma's sign and seed.

Shemshaun

Tenants of the instant when the cameras flash
and all is visible,
our names in the guest book,
in the common light.

I am a mystery like many another,
Like Finney's untold fault, or woeful K,
who could not crash the old town Castle gate.

A wounded mindman monk,
like the slight, stooped little master
of the headlight eyes,
light-blinded Joyce the comic warbler,
how he sang!

The bowed head, the upturned collar
against the cold blast,
that's him, that's our man!
the island-stepping, stone-slipping,
chill-darkened, heart-eaten,
thirsting, desert-treading lad.

His photo by Man Ray: the face in shadow,
leaning on an idle hand, is he really smiling?

His low, melodious laugh:
(it is my music) like a faraway surf,
a farewell, love-gone, world-lamenting
last judgment weather laugh
of darkest autumn.

Markhark the dark!

A shady character, I'd say,
a hidden smile, a glimmering
little private joke, diminuendo,
in a latinoirish lowlaugh twang,
what an actor!

The resting, soft curved hand,
the bowed brow, the tender drooping,
the tremble-twinkle of an eyelid,
the grief-lined smile.

The earthling, nightling, dawnling,
the airling, timeling, seemling.

Lucien Leclerque

Lucien, you were an encouraging sight,
your light-struck glasses, your head in the sunset
haloed like the burning bush.

I followed your "Journey To The Sun"
from the lowly start, the crack in the sidewalk,
to the lighthouse mirrors marching in a ring,
to the beam's sweep of the wrinkling sea,
to the horizon blaze,
the sky a storming dragnet

of seabirds streaking,
shooting the rapids of the air.

It was the bird's eye that did this,
that took this world-leap,
that drove its heart-beat, tracking up the sky
with its meaning and calling and continual cry.

Lucien, well named, light writer,
quick of eye on the wing,
you know, I've done time in the darkroom too,
under the ruby lamp, dim beacon,
wooing to presence
the waking image in the watery film,
to the selfsame luck of being,
of beating wing and flying moon
and all who leap free
of the ravening, ever-reaching enemy sea
to roam with me
once through the world.

Migrant

The truth will bring a man down:
what had cost Oedipus his eyes
or felled old Hemingway,
what mocked the white-haired papathetic breast
of the proud hearted, bloody-palmed fisherman
hounded by the shark
to his boundary beach;
warped vessel, shuttled ashore,
out of his time, untimely
stilled old man of the sea.

Bird

An old sky mariner
left the breeding flock for solitude.

Who knows what weighed him down,
what mourned, ached, drowsed there
where he lay and faded?

With what somber yielding
his serious, high, unsightly head
drifts with the snow,
and the bird of space consents
and lays his cheek on the world.

JUST ONCE MORE

Just Once More

The blooming of bees: a rumorous burning,
a numerous murmur of populated air,
a wing-strumming hither thither
from heart flower to flower heart loaded and pollen
     blown
honey drunk, sun drenched, noon time and dream time
gold and green time, pistil and phallustime,
where the bee sucks, and bursting full
and breastful Junetime.

It was a day for titillation
and for copulation and cohabitation
everywhere according to their habitat,
going about their business which was
their pleasure,
les belles atingalinging in the sun
and nobody lonely,
surfing and basking in skyblaze and in shady nooks
and cool of the evening, and with nightfall
having slept the day through to their heart's content,
with the starlight came all awake

And joined the cicada chorus,
the katytime waltztime zigzag ringaround and once
     more
and yet again and all together one long dringdingding,
on and on with the turning night world zing zing
and a chirp.

The brooks overflowing their mudbanks and rillrocks,
love thy rocky rills!
all the springs bubbling and trilling
down the slopes and through the rushes,
here and there a finch, a starling,
high-tails, arrows down for a quink a cool one
merrily down the throat and on our way.

And so it comes to pass,
the calling, the doing and undoing,
the mating, the parting, the offspring, one more spring,
and another turn, every good turn, what's fair is fair,
one more round, just this once, just once more.

Stone

Can't get away from that place!
it is my lodestone, my millstone, my stone in my side

Where I was mislaid
where I left my hoe
where I sat down by a stone
and it was my own, my vine-twined headstone.

And there my weathered head was heathered,
down to earth, a realist at last,
to do my share and plow my part
and enrich the ground of all,
bound to it, to my very boundary,
to the blade's edge turned
and a fertile loam to boot, enough for all
and for all time's care.

A straw man, a four square sign in the field

I would stand and stare,
and so the corn shoots cracked the sod,
the bean poles weighed until they popped
and all prospered awhile
through a summer season,
a scarecrow and a witness
that what was, was,
on the stalk and on the vine: a fable
told and retold
at every turn:

Sprung into being,
and on to the highway, homing to our acre,
we two, twain, aching for our own.

So centered, earthborne,
heavy from the hoe and the spade
and in the end
back to our thicket and our treasure vein,
hardened to it, until the lasting part
is crystal, coal and stone
to the ring of the blade.

A Toast to Mount Laurel

A draught of that bitter hill-brew:

From the rock side's flow
through the rotten leaf rust
and flinty ridge soil,

From the mountain slip,
the rift and sand sift,
and split quartz quarry,

From the cliff's brow,
the high ridge hovering,
and westward loam,

Where the rain gullies the roadway:

The good, vined hill
toils down the rocky fen
to the poison ivy wall,

To the gnat nest, the owl haunt,
the out-house rose bush,
the moonlit tangle,

Down to the reed-banked pool:

There, from the skyburst
the ripple rings start
and shiver and shake

The imaged night sky;
the life-stung gnats
spring to the leafage,

Seeking and swarming
to every space,
a cloud of stingsong,

Scattered, thistle-winged, world-blown:

To seed the dewdrop
and plant their offspring
in the horse's hide

And in the mouse's ear;
the earth is their nest
and motherside.

With all, all that has fled:

This quarry head of mine,
the flitbats haunting
this war-worn gnome,

This thrumming west-head,
reined and checked,
smacked and windsped,

Laurelled, hemlocked,
homeward, loamward,
doomward head.

A bitter hill-brew
to lay this stone to rest
in the green bed.

By A Lilac

By a lilac I happened on a pair of lovers:
two lettuce-green joycey grasshoppers
in flagrante on a twig under a leaf,
snug, intertwined, enwrapped and never stirring
in a day-long trance. I teased them with a grassblade
and Mr. Graceloper pulled up a long knee joint
and he was a sharp one. Leave us be, he said,
and the sign said: Do not disturb.

The Mites Of Spring

The furry and feathered, all over the place
are biting where it itches,
digging and drilling in their breast fuzz
or under their wing,
burning with those mites,
plunging into road dust and poolpuddles,
out of their minds and their skin and bones.

And the young pear tree is bleeding,
its jismjelly serum
crawls down the cracked sere barkside
to the very ground,
wounded to the quick
at the curled leaf tip
by those damned mites.

A Human Vessel

I ask, is was that me, could that have been?
it ain't youloo and it ain't melee!
something elseward and over now
and you can't pin it on me
I have an alibi lullabye.

The blundering past
in wartime, when man's home is in question
spared me in its night flight stride.

Could be somebody else,
could be tu, du, you.

Nothing but a song is all it is,
all imaginairy and has no teeth
so don't take fright, you can look now
it's only make-believe, a lofty sentiment
and slows in distance to a standstill,
through your glass you see
it is a human vessel, or perhaps a star.

"A status of the subject, overcast,"
poor old Coleridge muttered with a sigh,
ailing to the last,
gentle exile of the haunted eye.

The waking eye, opening from a dream,
alas, the seeking eye,
like a falling bird, returning
to its dark, to its eave and to its close.

Oh, the chances we took, who once had come to pass!
couldn't get along, so long! and you're alone,
the swarm of all occasions, known and unknown
all atone, all come to this:
cold in the sun, and naked as a stone.

A Something Like A Nothing

Like the vibrant point and stain
on the recording scroll of wave and weather,
the starlight writes your name
in the abstract, in the water of the eye,
wrathful eye, vacant eye, woeful iris,
world interpoint
of fateful inner and outer:
there, in a shiver at the crossing,

the sun-born, world-encircling pulse
from the crowned, shaggy parent,
King Sun,
regathers and converges to His image:
a black dot.

And this is the lucky donné, zoomed and assumed
and the start of it all.

Omit the axiomatic eye, and you lose
the ground, the zero point
of place,
and then, Oh say can you see?
so follow me and trace
this little parable that turns
on the spiral stair
of the DNA and RNA
and on reflection hath
a human face.

You are, and are so, a cosmic, a funny,
a something like a nothing,
a little spheric space, a seeing sphere
of sum and substance wide awake,
ever orient, ever tending,
in this dazzling sense
the worldly, the sensational
truth of the matter: that we are,
however come, however far,
the living dolls
of the energenetic
Sun
of Seeing
and Being
and Being Seen.

Ding Dong

1

Can't bear those faraway bugle notes
of that hateful world,
where I was a private in the mangy army
of Worldwar I.
I can't bear it, I tell you,
that Golgotha tingaling.

To think that here and now
it is tingalinging still.

What doth it profit, to be angels in this heaven
if we be childless, sprung without offspring,
and all that wearying were for naught,
and by that spite of all, it were to end?
And all that tending, rended and unhearted,
in the universal ding dong.

Oh, to be mercifully cracked
and hard of hearing from the flash,
to be blinded just in time
to see no more.

A superdupe collopsable catastrostroke,
big, big, so big in fact, no man may claim
credits in the opening flicker on the screen,
anonymous production, and none to blame.

Not even our Olympian spectators,
our ivory tourists on the Left Bank
with letters of credit in the foreign office,
when there was still a legacy, a little something
for any meanie left behind.

2

By flight, by sight,
by dead reckoning by night,
by that prophetic pain,
when business is bad, ding dong,
and the banks close down.

You are standing in line, waiting your turn,
and you are only one at a time, while they
are behind those closed doors
scheming to outface you.

Youman versus youman, man to mantis praying,
and eaten in the end, tingaling.

3

Ah, distant dying smile, how come, how gone,
that sensed and feared and now is astral past!
In that mute span is there no secret beat,
no breath to be and be reborn?
There must be, my darlings, yes there must,
by this mysterious circumstance,
that we are on the trackless seasonway
upon our soulstice tending,
by our yearning towardness,
our winged and soaring nature,
our outward knowing and our inwardness,
our topmost risings, our netherdowning,
our birding and wording, our flightiness
and restless nesting.

A FAR CRY FROM ADAM

Yankel

Who was he, and what about it,
that bitter taste, that sullen straining,
did you know him? isn't it amazing
that he was tolerated at all
(by the tolerant)—taken in a bit
and down a peg or two
and was noticed in certain places,
when there was room for everybody?

As it turns out in the light,
another one of those,
chastened to his measure and punishment.

All that turmoil
inside a little paper bag,
a skin and bones, a small plucked cockerel,
a plain little common man, is all,
is all there is. And there he stands,
a yankel, a yokel, a yenkiman junkman,
dealt in scraps and cast-me-downs,
every bit of precious offal
a gem of purest hoorah and eureka hooray!
invented everything all over again,
and discovered America.
A meddler and a peddler, alone and late,
rang his little bell from street to street
(the harlot's cry, and the ox in wrath,
and the dog at heaven's gate).

Charlie

By a farewell stroke of wit,
a lucky calamitous slip, departing Charlie
would drop the ultimate epigram,
and blow the whole thing,
in its own light the dire truth
so startling, it caught you
by your tear and your laugh,
it got you, didn't it!

On the postcard, x marks the spot
where he crossed the bar,
(riding the rails from bar to bar)
resting a foot on every corner,
without welcome or fanfare,
no key to the city, entering town after town
without a key.

But above all it was his crossing out
that was the historic point
of his pastime:
to war, woe-begone, and be gone.

Got a job and held it twenty years,
rose to V.P., signing papers,
the sign man who signed off
and was signed away and blotted out
by an advertising blotter.

Who would believe that this paragoon,
a round-eyed yearner,
a foreigner and one-time mariner,
could in his reach and range, come down
to such a lachrymouse, to this!
it proves he got around, and none so low,

none deeper than himself, and goes to show.

If you stop a minute I'll explain.
I'll tell you my story if you let me.
A solitary dime is all it takes,
for a whole life for a life for ten cents
in the big town with a heart
and a tear from the heart
on this coronary corney island.

Abiegandhi

"A party of one,"
"me and God," says he,
"what do you want,
a Party without a problem?"
Hello, Mr. Shelley, will you head our Party,
lead us to power?

How about *you?* would you choose to run?
Why not, who you think you are,
Ahandi Goosegandhi with your golden eggs,
above the battle and keep your nose clean,
afraid they'll call you what you are?

And put you in a barbwire chaingang
and spend the rest of your life
stir-crazy, don't you dare stir,
singing Old Man River,
in that tremendous, throat-throbbing
basso profondo.

Go out there on that limb
and hang for all we care, a lot of good,

not even a line in the obituary column,
who would send it in, and who
would come to your funeral?
if you had power, like a gangster,
with tons of flower horseshoes;
bare-headed mourners in the drizzle
and his beloved widow
follow the hearse
in single file, a mourning multitude
for a farewell look
at Lenilou Dostoilstoi Abiegandhi Lincohn.

Harry Carey

What makes you such a cockaroo,
startling old and brittle
in your sudden ways of being,
your hooked laugh and eagle glare?

Tossed out in World War One
for showing a foolhardy glimmer of brains
and laboring ever since, breaking himself,
alas to no avail,
for his talent was teaching and this was no way
to waste a man's powers.

When even the Party crossed you out
(that was a blow to stagger a Lenin)
a man without a school or a class
or a country or a committee or a comrade,
who left his wife and bed and board
for the hard lot and the bum's rush
to the lonely hall bedroom
and on to the flop house. A secret man

with no kin and no convert
and no Father. Why, even Jesus
had more than that.
The man's mad, of course, (and who is not?)
withering to behold.

Sam Links

A funny guy,
his hard-won, faithful little dogma,
fierce little hydrant header,
barking up the wrong tree,
and it would never do,
in politics or letters;
and so, a blessed relief
not to be called, not to report
nor join in approval or applause
nor render an account
in that ardoring and disardoring,
knocking about, disarrayed,
brother against brother,
in low uncivil disputation,
contending for what?

Raising the stars and stripes on a stick,
a committee of one to take a stand
for what and for whom, really?
for the way you feel,
for say can you see,
to dare and declare
and disturb your good neighbor

A confrontation:
the one in a brutish rage at subtlety,

the other in pale dismay at rude behavior,
(a mere misunderstanding)
the one wielding a club, and the other
a finger in a book,
so they came to blows.

From my sheltered height, in my eyeful tour,
above the battle, in a quiet hour
I can dream awhile, can't I? and review
the evils of our time.

In my mind's eye as I rove and uneasy lie
I see by the papers:

SAM LINKS IS IN JAIL

My friend of those early downtown bohemian pastimes
in the brownstone twenties and thirties,
who went to Hollywood. Well I remember him,
haunched, paunched, and jolly well met by noon
in the Bonalisa office where they had a monk's head
as their colophony mark. And there I would join them
for lunch by candle light, a gallant coterie
a goaty foreign quoterie
of intehellectuals.

And there it was that poet Sidney paled
as Lena made an entrance at the door,
slid from his chair and out of sight and mind,
subversed, a banished bard,
poor Sid, laid low
by romance and escapism,
presto with the antipasto, the vanished man!
out the back way, down the cellarway
to the sewers of Paris.

I saw your name on a streamer, Sammy,
in a May Day parade, and I see by the papers,
you stood up to those Senatories
and showed them your haunch in court,
they couldn't tempt or tamper
with a man of your stamp,
my hardy, true blue
ruddy uncle Sam! stood up and was counted!
so keep a stiff upper lip
and we'll show up at your funeral,
a Q.E.D. to demonstrate
our solidaridity.
And Sid will be there,
his moustache bushier and more unkempt
(really looks foreign, like a Conklin
a conked, slapsilly cross-eye
Charlie chap).

Be seated, gentlemen, Mr. Sam Link Lou
will be with you in a moment,
just one more layout to meet a deadline
and he'll be laid out in fond remembrance
and you may file past in single file
in memoriam of gory memory,
the way you treated him,
give him the brush-off, would you?
served him right,
and in the cold, cold ground.

Macmanx

Macmanx in newsprint gray,
sitting on the sidewalk
with mattress and spring in the air
and a cardboard tied with twine,
legs crossed, head in hand, self supporting.

India and China revere the wayside saint,
but here the villain on his haunch
is in disgrace. The headline cries:

VILLAGE POET OUT, RENT OVERDUE

Poor Poxmocks, they can't read.
And nothing shows in this bad print
on the front page of the *Daily Night,*
the poems you wrote, in the heat and in the cold,
as you lay on your cot, pencil poised;
the point would descend and the finger would write
and having writ you would arise
and condescend to the street,
sage old page-rager! many a sheet
you stained for your pains.

A gentleman of the press is calling
to put your picture in the paper.
Look at this guy, a card, a character.
Fellow poits admonished, deplored, abhorred,
called him pretentious and euphew fancy,
and they were right and to hell with him,
he made his bed right there against the curb.

As your old man used to say, *the blunt truth:*
you're headed the same way my friend,
where there's room to lay thy head,

every dog his day, never fear.
And then, suppose it's you,
conversely, in plain prose: calling for help,
does your old comrade cat Mickmock Macmanx
fly to your defense
and leap into the breach and bare his breast
and strike a blow? Ha wha!
or ever raise his ass from that pavement
to labor in a glass cage,
to sort mail or mop a floor
and be paid and pay off
so they'd let him stay in his room
and drop dead for all I care?

In this harbor city of ours,
I harbored this predator, now out on his ear,
in his dignity and rage for a better world
and his visionary manner depressive.
His lifetime of seeking, and the blows he took
in his staggering stride!
until a knee gave way, and a fallen arch,
and the migraine, the rheume,
the anthropoiditis, the suffering
of and from mankind.

By his integrity, crust, hootsbie and gall,
demanding of common man,
taking the hard road to oblivion,
by that odd seventh sense,
all expectation, to the fainting end,
that something would turn up,
by the curious hardihood
of the soft tissue and yielding fiber
and gray matter and the very bone,
the pertinent persistence,
the ear cocked for survival,
to the last frog-leg twitch,

until assistance came,
and your consistence is revived,
and you're yourself again.

Damn them all,
the way they eye me, catching sight of me
with a catch in their stride,
at my face in the first edition
and my scare-head: EVICTION!
Village Poet's Predilection For The Open!
A mighty man was he,
and an iron hand, and the sparks flew,
and he owed not any man.

It's the village atmos in this fearful town
that brought me down and out for a breath of air,
back to the thirties and even the twenties,
and that's what did it: undone by the times.

Observe this picture of me, a fargone star
in the New Yerkes past,
(though you'll find no trace of me
in the obit-you're-it,
for you're not around to read your own).
What's the idea, dragging things outdoors,
I'll call my lawyer,
give me just an hour to call, call around,
could do it for a nickel not long ago.
Oh say can you spare, a dime for a life,
one dime ten cents, a dime for a little more time
and a time for a dime if you have it,
and what did I do with it, and where's Moe?
Help, Moe, help, help!
they got my books, they got my papers,
my fame and my name,
and my purse and my trash.

So look at you,
what you've done to yourself, Mackmoey,
how did you ever, so fargone?
And look at me! Flat on my back in my pent house:
the two extremises of the premises
of our society.

Mickey, my poor mehicking drunken peon pot,
cold on the ground and out like a light
on the pavestone sidewrack,
what can I do for you my good man?

Reggie

He used to stand in rags
on the corner of Times and Tombs.
They found a million dollars
sewed inside his lining,
under his skin, in the armpits
and sacroiliac,
some of it was moldy
and the moths had got the rest.

Appeared on the front page
frayed and torn,
rolling down the subway aisle,
and trampled in the rush hour,
so the last trace
of his last race
was lost forever
in the trodden sodden.

Once on an autumn night,
I was walking along, alone,

as in a moony song,
when suddenly behind me,
the rustling of pursuit,
the drum of racing hooves:

It was Reggie in a hurry,
he was now a solitary
bone-dry skeletal oakleaf
dashing after me,
scurrying criss-cross after my scent,
rattling like a beetle shell
and leaping like a tortoise,
a starfish in a dive,
a crazy kite in a crash
down the dark shining street.

Ben Shahn's Miner

Come out from under there, you undergrounder,
where are you hiding? it's summertime,
come on out and sleep in the noonday sun
with mad dogs and Englishmen.

Is there a man down there?
He was frantic to get out of there.
Ben drew him on a white sheet,
up from coal shadow
with the black-rimmed eye,
the hombre staring back at you,
the hard guy you had angered for so long.

And his old lady with her babe in her arm,
too tired to push away
a wisp of hair in her eyes

or blow it away with a puff
on this hot day.
Ben drew her waiting at the mine,
and wept her into dark and bright
and brighter still and fierce in sight to be
in diamond light forever known.

Miss Moore

Nonesuch Marianne,
spare, spunky, apple-tart,
tuned like a tinkling brook
to surprises of stony terrain,
fresh as a rainbow,
brave as a meadow thistle.

Who could have foretold her,
from childhood hymns and homilies,
legendary Marianne,
angel of elucidation,
charitable to a nobody,
undaunted
by "pedantic literalists,"
unimpressed
by "the simulated flight upward,"
and quick to exclaim: "what is strength?"
and "all are naked!"

In her own, her native land,
unread by the millions
(not one in ten thousand
knew a line of her verses),
content
to cheer the Dodgers from the bleachers,

and accepting with grace
the crown of video fame:
to toss out the first ball
in the World Series.

Head high in the holiday air,
the tender girlish cheek
in the rosy shadow
of her ageless chapeau,
as the man out in left field
declares to the Sunday world:
"Miss Moore has class."

Patriarch

Shudder in the cold, raging at cabs and buses
plunging past the black mirror-depths,
the night wind as wolfish here
as on the open plain in the Russian winter
of War and Peace, where I arrived by the magic
of a Sunday paper photo of Tolstoi,
at sight of which, tears brightened Sylvia's eyes,
for she was still in mourning for her mother,
whose dream-self had been Anna Karenina;
as a Polish belle she had worn a gown like hers,
wasp waist, broidered satin, frothy lace,
in disarray across the cruel rails
glistening to the horizon.

The paper apparition of Tolstoi
sits in a flat of the immutable past
and endures like Bergson's cinematic time;
he is seen full-face in Russia,
a pocked moon over a streaming cloud of beard,

a monumental ghost in a frock coat,
the gnarled hands clasped
in burdened Christian repose,
and deep in distance through the shaggy brow,
an angry eye! that has spoken and is mute
in the dark of Abraham's bosom.

Name Please

That's me in there,
in and out of it, marxing time, lost in the lowlife,
dogsick, going from doc to doctrine, masking myself:
what's wrung wit you?

Mainly eye trouble and loss of voice
as if each breath were your last, and not a sound,
for you can't see in this light.

If somebody asked, where would you be then,
your name please, well, your name,
who you think you is was, your name,
Izzyloo or Samloo by chance or mischance
as may very well could be?

A snob you turn out to be, in that tweedy turnout,
between those swinging mirrors, frontview, profile,
rearview and how is it around the shoulders?

Gaining weight, from waiting, waiting around,
temporizing, tempered by the time,
the perpetual Monday Marne
of Worldwar One.

An adman signman from way back, a stoop appearing

so the neck slants forward, lucky dog,
well draped like a roman emperor,
approaching middle age, a slow walk down the aisle
to join the hellders.

A fine figure of a friggerer, so well turned out,
is it that guilt becomes him
or is it rather unbecoming, unseemly,
his going, his passing, his undoing?
unbutton it and have it sent.

Could your own frail bones support you
all day long between those mirror walls?
or is it worse or worsted
or a finer quality wool or cheviot or twill
or wooster yet than the hours you spend
drear-hearted over the drawing board?

A little squatter-qitter
so mannerly in his mislaboring
to his daily quitting time.

The Sign Man

I appear from a hole in the world,
ungrounded early on an afternoon,
a burrower and tender ender
coming up for light and air,
a half-man, a half-a-day man
     (a) profile
     (b) fullface
a semi-presence in the offing,
partial to absence,
each day creating and departing

and sufficing for the day,
in short, the five-foot-seven sign man
of an ad house. It is called a house,
though but a bit of space within a bit of Space,
petitioned off, pettily marked off
by a seller of   space
of these United Estates,
a two-bit two by four
paced off from East to West
on this outer deck of the Earth,
a corner on the heaventh floor,
up-up to a self-levelling stop
and a window glimpse of the Hudson.

This sighing Sinbad with his angles
and his sinus and his clogged condition,
on a dull sunless morn
weeping or mourning at his work
or summing up a breathless meditation,
as if he were the weather man
of the signs
and marks and darks
and bounds of being.

Manicle

How come you imagine you're going places,
a guggenheimer gogonner homer,
with approval from above?
you'd be in irons if truth were told
and down in the hold safe and secure,
so stop dreaming, it's not for you,
you're a bee in the hive, a humbody,
a humbug hatched in season where you belong;

and besides you have no pride,
way over on the left in low company
laughing like loons over their coffee
in all-night cafeterias; what's to laugh?
why, when you're talking to Tony Dario
suddenly you got a Talian accent?
waving your hands like you were him
or his twin brurr?
so empatic, sympotish, should live so long,
the invisible man!

The heroh of the erah, hurray for you,
a hactor with an ackhack,
a low comic with a high nose,
and your heels go clackety on the sidewalk,
tiptap to any tune,
rhythm in your baggy pants, ha!
and ha! springtime and simhes torah
in de hazen.

And can you sing,
hey mister what can you do
with your belly button your
umbiblical bellicle
billiken begatgut?

Why sure enough, son, I can contemplate it

And give meself such a turn
and such another turnabout
and turn meself inside out
and ex a cute roundabout
backspring.

The Hypochondriac, An Old Print

Seated in the foreground,
hugging a little dachshund to his breast,
and in the shadows a huddle of physicians,
whispering, with backward glances,
as he smiles like the Mona Lisa;
he's way ahead of them, and they are way behind,
and they are baffled all right, the laugh is on them.

Gazing upward and inward, like a blessèd demoiselle,
ineffable, inviolable, sphinx-like, and as hard
as a pyramid or a corpse.

Made his will and left them his all,
for it's all in le monde: all his ills illusory,
like a mondrial chondrial vision
of T. B. and no can see, or leprosy,
or an unnamed virus,
filterable, alterable,
disturbed by light, transformed
by the mere fact of being seen,
for its being is inimical to being seen,
is diagnosed as antignostic, is reversed by prognosis,
so that an exploratory reaches the outer air,
and all is open to hypothesis.

And that is why the good gray doctor
is so secret and so gray,
and takes a nip of nightshade
to return to reality, for he's in deep,
and philosophy is not his forte;
and he'd better keep his insight out
and his outsight in,
if he knows what's good for him
and wants to stay around awhile.

Thank you doctor, goodbye doctor;
and you go out to breathe again
and say Ah! to the world,
a deep breath of the living; for a moment
you almost thought you'd never,
a new leash on life, the old dog's back
and at it again.

But it was not to be, and not for him,
what can you do with a ragbag sag like that?
came home to lie down and his eyes are closing,
not much here to breathe its last,
nor ask the reason why; let it die down and lie;
tiptoe out and close the door with care.

All Cats Are Mortal

His tufted ear, alert to east, alert to west,
showed the coral earbone, curled like a snapdragon.

His eyes blazed tenderness, devoured me
with a yawn of pearly fangs.

Caught a wishbone to toss and rattle.
Scat! I cried, you ratty old Bat!
and he froze in mid air,
tough Timmy Tomtut
with the fierce markings,
angelic and warlike,
marching off and settling down
to meditate and wait
and get me in the end.

A trim little man
in the shape and form of a Cat.

Here's a case of Timtom, item T:
entailing (as a cat a tail)
Me, a tale-bearer out of school
to catch a notion
and have a fling at it.

How like a monkey, leaped from wall to wall,
crouched by my door on nature's errand,
like the little fiend in the field
I had seen once in the mating throes,
deep as the farmer's mare that shuddered gaunt,
head turned and flaming eye,
in such another suffering.

Tommytiddle,
with no foresight and no hindsight
in your pretty head,
avowing your solemn cause,
your presence and purpose:
to love and to eat,
who slept your life away
between crescendos of hunger
and lay down and dozed off
into self-forgetting bone and fur
which blew off into thistled air
and nowhere a sign of you
to honor your little nose
lively with news
when the world still concerned you,

And gave up and lost interest
in being,
and were no more engaged, and were excused,
and were free of the coil, the catgut, the fiddle string,
Timmy my little tomfool,
my titmouse Tammy.

Deadbeat

All overboard, and then, ashore,
they rolled him in the shadow of the Bridge.
My british, yiddish, brackish
Louie McLonely.
My Coney Island harkbarker.
My Sasha Pisher Pasha.
My pitchy, seasoned, blacksea Sonny.
My little seashell.

A boned and stripped and marinated hadlad
hooked and hacked with the cough
with a crackalack alassitude.

Rounded the Cape
and clear across the Equator tossed
a farmer boy asea and awash.

That was my dapple-faced boy
a low loon, a chiney din dinney
a caller and recaller, a farringer
a far cry from Adam.

A grodno gborney horney polak.
A fictive Lawrence troglo, that he war too,
a wary hairy high-combed cockalaroolou.

A timitive primitive
in his tumidity, his homorigidity,
his hamadried humor to be tumid
in his curiotimid way.

A dhirty liar, a sinbard with his tales
of hobogobs and headhaunters.

The cannibalou, the honeylooloo hannalou,
the saint louie blueboy, cyanic
deadbeat Lou.

That's him on the numbered passport,
left profile, right profile, foolface
identifee fi fofum, an icky
idification, by his micky-dickie
that he was circumcized
and circonflexed and hexed and next in line.

And descended by his hairedity
from the old sangfroid beards of ire,
bards of a Father.

Sailorboy ashore,
sailed to his girl in port,
to kiss and part and away with him,
the bum he ever was, wherever
he roomed and rammed,
winning all the world wars
and coming home some day.

Yes that's him, I'd know him anywhere,
do with him what you will,
guilty as hell, Lord we are unworthy.

A nice thing to say of His handywack
and wrack and rune!
back where he come from, seasilly, flat on his back
without a buck, und in ein blick, in a flick,
he's gone, fargone, the gamey thing.

FIRELAND

The Invention

1

The prevailing wind
of long journeyed mutterings
flows through our pent house in the sky.

A warplane squadron outward bound
ascends, engulfs and darkens us
and storms the horizon, trailing
this drone of dread.

On the approach a waspish note
sang in the motor roar, I knew it well,
it was like the viper's sting
which in my puffed flesh once had said to me:
"See, nothing's easier than dying."

Or like the glitter of the spinning shaft
when the drill press snarls.
I had been cautioned: bear in mind the tale
of the novice with the ample shock of hair,
dreaming at his work, who screamed awake
at the sly, whirling touch, and tore away,
and left his bloody scalp in the machine.

And once I saw a bee-swarm on the wing,
that sang the same motor whine
as this cold bitter thing.

You heard it in the warplanes raging down,

the leap of acid fury murder bent
and on the loose in the sky.

This sound is wound about so many ways,
so many matters of fact, should we despair?
though it is only a shaving off the lathe,
(and the lathe has been turning for aeons).

2

My head drilled on, by night it speeded up,
each part in turn was whirred and shot away.
One of these days you'd blow a filament,
then darkness, silence, peace,
smiling in his sleep, poor dear, so young,
hardly a few thousand and one nights
to his body and soul.

Don't distract me,
right in the middle of a problem,
come back later, some other time,
don't keep breaking in, go away.

What's he about? Don't be too sure
you've got him, marked your man and pinned him
        down.
What's this, what have we here?

A dipter adaptera, a contriving fly.
A flimflam artificer in a jam.

The damn thing flies alright, but will it sell?
There's the rub, sir. What are you going to do,
there's a diophantine fog about this diaphane,
the optical art, the light and sight entail
high operational skill.

Fantastic, fabulous, millions in it, they'll steal it,
don't you dare show it to your lawyer!
What do you know about shady deals on the Street,
lurking bulls, bears, wolves, lions,
horny unicorns? Can you hide it,
embed it in graphite? deploy it in warfare,
or in the ars of peace? Is it subversive?
Can it go back where it came from?
Don't touch it! look, it's alive!

See what I made with ciphers,
marks and renderings, limn by limn,
from the mind's eye to the foundry castings
to the turnings, to a tolerance
of plus or minus point oh, oh, a millipoint,
calculating every stress
by a mere straining of the eye,
and proved it in the light of day
by a flip of a switch,
and without a cent of my own,
and owed not any man,
wet with honest sweat of the brow,
a mental giant proletarian of the brain,
lisping in numbers, littered and belittled,
and dropped, dead broke, and cracked clear through.

This trying, this expense of heart and main,
and persons unnamed, touching this artifice,
drawn by rumors and mongerings each to each,
to a tale of schemes and schemers
intending and contending in a world
unknown to me, too slow, too late
to see what had been done
by whom to whom,
the right, the wrong, the dire loss of it all.

"A shining patent lights you to a lawsuit."
Look at Moses Deforest, forty years
in a wilderness of sewers and pursuers
of the passages, the tangles of the law,
and lost every time he won a case in court
till, worn and wan, with millions in the bank,
millions for all, he died a broken man.

And you fancied yourself
an artificer, Jimmie Deadaloss,
with a mere pen in your artifist,
dedallying with whirds! Did you ever
drop a mercury lamp?

Glass flies in air,
quicksilver mirror-balls go scurrying
to all the cracks in the floor,
and another you, each in his little sphere,
looks back at you, returns your stare.

TRIAL AND ERROR

1. Witness

It was judgment day
and each would be first
when his name was called
in the great pillared chamber,
the doubled whispers twanging far and high.

As we lay there in various attitudes of dying
among the morning papers, no one stirred.

Turn me over, turn me on my right side,
for it hurts me so. Good grief, what hit you?
Let's have a look, there's a good lad.

It's the eyes, I have gone blind,
not blind enough for a seeing eye dog,
for I am not an alcohecco homonomynous,
and, so help me, I may never be called.

The issue here is vision,
a matter of means, of the visionary means:
for intending, or attending, or merely tending,
for inlight and outsight, for largeness and horizon,
as a man of means, numbered among the numbered,
name on file, offspring of an offspring,
among the living, among the visible.

For the afar, for the tiny cloud in the sky,
for seeing and for knowing and again for weeping,
there is in the eye an ever welling source,
and a dew forming and the birth
of the bright offspring, the eye-like tear.

2. Exhibit A. Sustained

We are now in Part II, Supreme Court, State of New
    York, by God!
I swear I never dreamed I'd be in the very trial room
where I lost my head, so help me, raise your right
    hand.

This is the public place, the forum arena,
the right side up, the outside of the inside world,
and in fact this is where the fact is and comes to light.

In this upper space, there is a fading out, a distancing,
in the cold light that shines the same on all,
and on the Elevated railway urinal
of vitreous porcelain.

On this fateful day of our Lord
nineteen hundred and whatever it is, on this
    sleepy-eyed morning
my distinguished adversary will break a lance or two,
heads will roll, the witness will sweat, the inquisitor
will turn, his lip will curl, his teeth will show
as the eye leaps to the jurors' faces.

It concerns a shipment of meat to Israel *via* the Horn,
riding high with half a million bucks, a strictly
    kosher deal:
for the people of the good book, the first born and
    the hindmost,
the poor Jewish people, by free enterprize,
a cold cut proposition. "Now gentlemen,
would you go by the facts, cleave to the facts
and the cleaver in evidence, never swayed
by sentiment, by bloody example and/or blood
    money?"

"You mean the learned rabbi Father Dunn
and two and twenty choirboys chartered a plane
to the port of embarkation, there to bless
the hindquarters of a traifer shipload?"

"Objection, your honor."
"Sustained."
"Sorry, your honor."
"And you swear they never (no sir) never delivered?"
Hysteria in the courtroom.

"And you flew to the port of Haiffa?"
"And you had a nice trip?"
"Sustained."

A plague take each and all! the riggers and hookers,
the schemers, contrivers, connivers, liars, denyers. Stained.
A dry-lipped, dead distaste, an over-all sourness. The balky
witness will not cooperate. Prod the carcass forward an-
other step. Stalled again. Stained.

Cadaver faced, silent, cornered, tongue-tied and quar-
tered, hollow eyed, reeking sour, revived, again revived,
damp wrung, the witness denies, refuses, guilty as hell.

And the verdict goes in his favor; who is without
guilt, the first stone, hell, somebody had to win. Rewarded,
blessèd are they, the salt and the sour, to make the desert
bloom. Fingers in half a million dollars, a hundred thou-
sand clear, split it four ways, plenty for all, Amerika,
goldeneh land, from ocean to ocean, amen, with the thanks
of the Court.

3. Exhibit B. Identifiction

Doris is home alone. The doorbell rings. It's a little stranger slob, a saggy lumpendreg, a vague pale nobody in a cheap suit and bow tie. As he stands there in his stoopy snoopy way, with his flat face and his fallen arches, someone behind him in the shadow points a finger at Dora. "That's her," she says.

Finally on the court calendar: ré: George Roy, M.D.,
né George Pillberg, recently of Budapest.

In a trice we've had our say; and the villain and his
    gang,
huge in bursting triumph, stride past us. Free!
Free! in die goldeneh land, Amerika ganif!

Really, it's all over and done with.

His sister, the trigger girl, the frigger-finger girl,
had pointed her out, in the matter of the adversary,
"her husband the doctor,"
in proof that she was she, a clear case
of another Ophelia drowning,
she crept into bed alone
for the rest of her days; and he no doubt
has since improved his bedside manner,
a smiling villain, he swore allegiance, and now is free
to point and finger and probe without fear or favor,
with a wary eye out for subversives, in the A.M.A.

So don't cry and don't yield to that little tremor,
that ain't-faint, want to lie down.

Should you knife your way in,
in a dextrous turn of a twist of the screw of the wrist

with your surgical skill would you sew it up quick
and back to daylight and bygones and on to the next?

What do you make of it,
what is there, what comes of telling,
in the rehearsal of it what do you find?

Is there anything in it, for any of us,
and how would we know, unless
we tried and were tried?

Poor Dora, sheared and parted,
in a mere moment, atom of history.

Do not scoff at the ancient bard in the old tongue,
what have you here but a change of air and range,
wherever you are? and dare not call yourself happy
upon your arrival in a golden land,
where all's fair in love and war.

Gone off, the false-face triggery,
the tracked down lowdown, fallen,
fled away, only the name there,
uttered and tittered and no one answers,
tinkled and tingled for another, no one there,
not a trace in the air
of that hasbeen who never was,
the voiceless mockery, all made up
to look like a man,
but not a sound in his sound,
not around,
he ain't around no more.

That was one way to be damned, he had damned
        himself out,
out of presence, out of hearing, out of our ways,
one to another, interwoven amongst ourselves,

belonging in our longings for one another,
in continuity by contiguity, the closer we come,
and our lingerings beyond our passings
through our own, our selfsame kith and kin,
presence and absence being but our modes of sense,
each called, clasped, clinging, though with farewell
    kisses
we go and are gone.

4. Exhibit C. They Saw It All

And the poor man stands agape,
now see what you did to the man,
he can't remember.

This is Al's day in court. A hoodlum ex-pug mauler,
the stone hauler from down the hill
had hauled off and knocked him down
among the square-cut stones.

A tremor all over, frozen silent,
stiff with fear-filled eyes, play dead,
and dare not draw thy breath in pain, absent thee,
like the little beast on the fieldstone fence, so tame
with banging heart, in death-like trance.

Then and there, at sight of silent Al,
I ran to the stone mason by the wall
and seized the pointed hammer from his hand,
and so armed I turned and great with rage in the field
surprised that prize rock hauler.

The hen leaps out like a fighting cock,
red eyed cackle fury, feathers flying,

the little chippie shrieks before her nest,
there's a great racket in the tree,
what a commotion,
dirty work at the crossroad,
and they came to the dark tower
and did the deed and done.

And I went for him, and lashed him down the road
to the crossing, but actually I was crying for mercy,
a begging hero, striking at this bully bastard
with my little hammerpoint, futile and impotent,
worse, still worse! for it wasn't
Al's grievous swollen face, rising from the rocks,
no, it was only that he called him and just because
he called him a Jew, that I wept and roared
and swung my little hammer.

Al found his voice and gave voice,
and he pointed his long arm at him.
"Now you've done it!" he cried.

The telephone lineman by the road
saw it all,
and his husky helper saw it all,
and the truckman,
and the stone mason by the wall,
he saw it all.

But when the state trooper drove up,
one looked east, one looked west
and nobody saw.

We came to the county court house
and there, waiting their turn,
his race and kin, salt of the earth,
sat in a row and showed
the hostile side of the face.

From the platform with the crossed flags,
his name is called,
the man comes up and is sworn.

And suddenly there he stands,
the warrior chief,
and there he stands the warrior chief
and there he stands.
Deaf and mute
and lost his mind, your honor,
can't think of the word, the bon mot.

If the sentence were suspended, another chance,
his wife is going to have a baby.

That night his old man's truck roars up our lawn.
Slam goes the truck door, out hops his old man.

"You know what they done to your kind over there,
that ain't nothin' to what we got in mind,
you'll see a thing or two, you'll learn a thing or two,
before we're through!" cried his old man.

Fireland

1

An unsteady sound below there, a quaver in the sigh
all illusion, all steam, issuing up into nowhere
and rain passing in a white fog.

The floods rutting the roads,
washing away the loam of our acres
and the columns of mercury falling,
the wagon-loads of homefolk
treking toward the uplands
to the world slum,
abandoning the cracked, the besotted,
the floating, the stranded,
and their drowned and dead.

And from the cellars, their heads emerging
in the light, the after-stillness, oh, look,
what's all around

Everywhere derailed, deranged, unroofed,
undone, let's leave all this behind,
let's not turn back, let's pray.

We prayed in our breathing, in our pores,
our poorbodies aching
with our striving away from there.

And whithering we know not
and do not suspect and have no plan
nor are we good schemers
though forever scheming
but good lackers, forever lacking.

How will the little ones grow, into what, in the mill
        towns,
in the Eastside, Southside, Loopside, lopsided
in the guttertowns? What sort of weathering
in in store for the kids, will they go to school and
        belong
to the white collar classasses, will they be kicked
        around
until they kick around their own, beating up the
        neighbors,
will they be dreaming of the fields blown off
in the dust cloud cyclone,
crying in their sleep?

2

What's going on down there?
Hot clouds and steel on stone, sparks and flames.

In his darkness the masked wasp-man
with quaking fore-arms, scarred and blue tattooed
steams and rattles,
his thrusting power drill screams
and dances in the death-dust
in the horny worldskin
the earthstone epiderm
and vapors pour up into the city air.

And a sturdy crop-head shoulders up from a manhole.
Our sailor boy is back, with a bad back
and a hole in the head.
Helmet screwed tight, down he went,
into the savagery of the sea,
weighted against the heavenward surge
to rise again and report
how he had fared below.

Below, beyond the slow sewer flow
sea-crawling to the nether nightfields
our common-tending fellow-fate
mingles in that outward, seaward traffic.

Under the underground, the turbine world,
the humming wires and braided cables
and at the switchboards the ear-phoned maidens
dreaming of Mardigras

Of girl squads prancing in time,
don't you love parades?
trumpet blare, fife obbligato,
drumroll and heartbeat,
thrillfrills and ribbons in the air,
and the cops on their throbbing cycles
waiting for the signal
to leap and roll.

One night on Broadway I heard the crying siren call
like a night cat on the loose. The traffic lanes part wide
for the maskmen roaring past,
the heavy-treading hearse-like long sedans
wheel round the dark
and dwindle to their distant fate.

The power-churned engines race away, rolling
with history, with the swift dark turning Iser,
with the Rhine, with the Steppes, with the Tiber,
with the Thames and the tolling London tower.

The hip-gunned blackguard bucks loll in their
        limousines,
smoking big black cigars. Why does the President
travel like a gangster?

3

A mere remark on the dazzle of Spring, a word on
      the weather,
and here you go into this Abombing and Abooming
and death on wheels, and the story in the papers
of the 27th Device
in Arizonia.

We are but isle madhatter smatterhorns,
with this old manhattanitis
in our sinus souls,
all suffering this same westland,
all pervious, gassed, airborne.

Who knows where you'll be next?
in straits as ever, as narrow
through all your marrow,
you harried little horrorman.

The flat tops are riding the moonsilver waters
where salt old Walt had his wits about him,
and a thing or two to say
about Demos.

Hi, Toots! how's my boy,
grown up to such a great big bambyman,
bristles on his jaw, down on his lip,
sprouting curly chest and pubic secret,
can't down and can't hide, sailor boy
of westward hoe and golden tideland.
You'll sail away and we'll never
see you again.

Little Bopeep in the big town,
just this once, what the hell,

the yolks at home won't know!
it don't show on your nose, so here goes!
whoops, another round, this one's on me.
Petrified, pie eyed, stiff,
tending tonight, on what grounds?
On any grounds. They lay you in the end,
they cockadoodle screwdloodle
lay you in the cold cold ground.
Leave it to the boys who know,
suckled in the deep Sow,
in a white spired sepulchre.

From stockyard, yardarm
and short arm inspection,
in droves came the humankine,
following the tinkle of a bell.

From summertime belltower boomtower
on a blooming Sunday morning,
a ringer dinger morning,
Ah Am, the great What Am:
a worldly, world-wide grin, a grim grin to all,
Massa Massaiah,
for all the world like a human!

The footsore boys dig in on Akrean soil,
and there they save and are saved,
spinning on a million TV screens,
where are they now? where the bombsight
thinks and follows and finds its target.

The flame thrower wears that thing
on his back:
Its churning, moiling tongue will sing
magenta to cyan to violet,
the cerement asbestos hands
will aim at what they aim to do,

the spectral dragon tongue
will leap with its prey
to the invisible.

The shame aim does that done deed
in foreign hill and town,
and the earth folk fold in flame,
and folk no molk,
no milk of humankine.

Oh bloody history,
in your hindsight the goggled flyer boys
drop their bursting black rosettes
on the beauty a world away below.
And yet by what mischievous trick
here to the naked eye, all is invisible,
but you in there arguing, making a deal, the devil
    take,
and what's the take, what's in it for you? us? eh?

Don't answer, the guy's cracked with the drought.
Caught in a draft and blown away
to Krea with the Krealists,
the maskmen with the bomboms,
the dark dingdongoliers

They break wind as they sow and reap abroad,
across the acres, the cruel archers
of the whirlwind: floods, tearfloods
their only answer,
tossed and crossed, and know not what
they have undone.

The man's been robbed and badly beat up,
confused and scared, reduced to odd devices:
crossing himself, kneeling and springing up,
arm raised to avert a blow.

Where are the men of good will
to outweigh the withering powermen,
Oh for a hope-ray
to steer the starry sohowl
of man's stormy nature!

Scared to death of man,
a rangerman of old, drives all before him,
a reacher, he'll out-reach you and teach you,
racked and wracking his way,
kin and enemy and jailor keeper,
roused from his sleep, watch out!
though on a nice summer day
the most amiable of beings,
tame and loving to his own,
and good to his mother.

A waropter, flyworm with fangs
to defend and devour,
the beast of the worst,
from tallest and highest
to the tail of the lowest,
out of his shadow, hurt and soil,
towering and glowering.

You been fooling around
with Walt and with Harry Thoreau?
What did they know of the arsonalia
of econicomical demockery
on fire to liberate the goons
of the ends of the earth?

Watch it, my boy, it don't pay to take chances.

You don't look like a native
of these parts,
why don't you

go back
where you cumfum?

Or climb those ancient heights where they fought it
      out,
the martyrs at the crossings, and it's okay now,
in a cloister nice and quiet,
or dingdong overseas to a black peasant
with a secret packed in his heart, and a popgun
aimed at you.

Pretty nearly tripped, bit by a dogma
right in your fannytickle pollytalk,
could give you rabies, all that rabbidical
opiate of them asses.

You were right, Percy Byssche, 'tis the poitry of old,
ringing from the Capitol.

What to do, shall we try the laboratory?
will they let us in? do we speak the language?
can we read a linear equation?
mathematically just an old dreck,
and lost our bearings.

And here, le pauvre philosophe,
what do you think he did?
He fell right through the hole of his torus,
it was too great a leap
from kabbala and torah
to torus, and down he went,
and they slammed the door
on the fallen toreadorus.

On the map theorem he moped into a decline,
and learned a lesson in topolingo.

His problem, to untie his tongue, too long in cheek,
and speak, though he stumble, grumble and complain,
but speak, if he would, if he dare, and be
a birdman nightingale,
a harbinger, a mournful imager, and speak, but speak!
Come, man, breathe and speak.

AN EYE IN THE SKY

THE PARTY

1. The Way It Went

It was as they were leaving that we heard the tolling,
the Isthmus bells. They went and we were spent,
and now it all rhymes, the high rent,
the lofty living room, bedroom and shower,
the party over and a sense of doom, of war,
here too as everywhere, war.
For my lifetime was wartime
and all were avenged, for faraway reasons.
The youth of the land came down like the wolf
and swarmed through our smart apartment.

And who cares who and what they were,
their names their incomes the things they said
and what they did to one another?

What if they did come and go,
what is it to you and me
who waited and greeted them
and stood dumbfounded as they fled?

2. Calling and Falling

She had a wily sidelong way and gave you a quick
    look,
She was a catty thing, a skinny tammaniny
and I didn't like her,
I had been mean to her and kind to her
and either way was wrong,
and even on a cold day or a dark day
she might curl up in a corner
and doodle out a riddling piddling
wiggle waggle, a sigma phrigma hi,
a foggy, icky, tacky, tricky
purring little poim.

She had a bony phony face
and a telltale hear: and those pretty boys
she brought to the party, yes,
she had a way of appearing

And here it is daylight again
and I am back in the wrong
just when things were almost coming out right,
coming into sight here and there.

And Leo is way off course,
out of touch, no good at all,
for he was the last of his line
and had no issue of his tissue,
following his calling,
calling and falling, falling "from dawn to noon"
and fouling up the lines as he fell.

After all that had befallen in twenty years and more,
when I called him up, all he said was:
"What do you want?"

It was my idea
to review those insults and hostile acts
and the ways I had been surprised
in love and in war.

When all were crying peace, peace,
and likewise love, love,
cathoholics alcoholy,
and the nameless, the cats and dogs
the unwashed and the unlovely,
every damn fool was saying love, love.

3. Quietly Close The Door

Myrtle sat on our deep green couch
and curdled up in it, with her sour smile.
"Moe," she breathed, "have you been here long?"
and her eyes ran a quick flick
around your living room in the sky.

What is she dragging around in her voice? what is the
burden of her sound as she moves around? and do you
have the nerve to tell her off and turn her out? what's
going on, what kind of a party is this anyway, do you be-
long to a Party? Art is true and we're wise to you, so on
your way!

And look who turned somebody out, who drove a soul
from your door! Swing wide the door and rush out and
shout into the night:

"Come back, come back through my door,
why, oh why, oh,
I never did such a thing!"

To tell the truth, it was they who ran off,

after a very brief call,
it was they who wouldn't stay
and skipped to another party down the street
and left us flat
in our quiet little coldwater flat,
within our four walls, on the floor in our shift,
with our cold feet on the bare floor,
sitting and crying.

You know what's really going on: the rumors flying
about the spacemen selling space, and about you!
so close the door gently,
and don't you of all people go slamming doors
for you know what's very likely to happen:
the lease running out on Liberty Street, and you,
free again, in the open, out and around,
so quietly close the door.

4. Myrtle

Her little frame hunched in a deep chair,
her bloodless face inert and blind,
with a wicked twist to her lip
as she feebly joined in applause,
clapping her weary, silent hands.

All very interesting, and why start trouble, really
how far could you go in a showdown,
and what did you want?

Carry a big sign: FAKE! Go to your studio
and letter that word in your own inimitable script
with a brush dipped in solid gold india ink
and autograph it in your golden hand.

Get yourself a pair of high stilts,
like a sandwich man, wear a mask and a sign,
and go and dare,
lay your head on a pillory, like a Puritan father,
hang your head in a stock, and sleep it off
in the public square, a man of the world,
a highwayman, a guttermutter, in the public eye,
and mud in your eye as they say at a party.

5. A Touch Of Fame

How odd for that man with the glitter in his eye
to come up and swear you were a born writer
and smile when he called you that, and knew you
for the man you were, the indefinable something,
je ne sais, genius?

So what, so you were famous Amos,
by the thyme of syne,
and iggle a mickle in it
for you or pour moi,
pas de toot, and a pain in me eye.

And what is fame, if you ask me,
for once upon a tyme
I had me youth and me health
and a touch of femme.

A brass band and ticker tape and City Hall?
You couldn't take it! Look at poor old wacky Max, he
      had it,
and look where he is now: the same old rat
in the automat; and those hoods coming round
for anecdotes and taking notes.

6. Sere and Mellow

And now I can't recall a single one
of that multitude of flurries and frenzies,
that snowfall of ideas,
it's over,
and worse than ever, if you ask me.

A pretty girl admired his voice:
"A sweet briar patch in a breeze,"
"a taste of wild honey,"
"a brooding, waking sound,"
and the old dear was struck dumb
and nearly fell over with surprise.

Years in the dark unloved, and all along
your voice was music to a girl:
like a sunburst, whole again!
like singing bees, wild honey, Iokanan,
wanted, loved and known
by one who was lovable and young,
smiling into your eyes
and opposing you with a smile.

Like high tide and full moon
and sudden song (a long story)
and a long way around to the truth
which was old and out of character
and what nonsense!

For he's a jolly good fellow
sere and mellow
with a blast and a bellow
and down the hatch.

With enough to retire,

with what it would require,
a winning number,
a ticket around the world,
just for two.

Funny how all of a sudden
nicht mir nicht dir, it was old age.

And now he's way out yonder in the dead past,
the silly old thing, and nuts to him and his kind!
nuts and wild honey, and nothing but brambles
in the wilderness of the past.

Way out yonder,
like the Eskimo who walks away
to lay his lamenting bones
on the bitter crust of the sea,
to return and partake of the world
by dispersal, by becoming a multitude,
each part going its own way,
to travel and mingle with the world.

THE SUBWAY

1. To Come Through

In your bright-lit shuttle, flying the tunnel maze
of the coal blue inside of the world,
straining for a sign
to tell you where you are, good lord,
headed straight for hell
for the outer county flats, the dead end plain
and the end of the line.

Cross at the next stop and hurl yourself back
like Lucifer, fly like a bat
fly blackface on your back,
home to your couch or your rocker on the hill

After riding about so long
where the train was taking me
past a name in mosaic on the porcelain wall
in this land of my fathers:
blurred figures of I know not what,
characters odd and even, the R backwards,
signifying heaven knows.

A brick dwelling on a desert street,
a snatch of a tune of long ago
and a tear in my eye from the wind.

"Poor Moe is so distracted,"
a friend would say with that unfeeling laugh
of health and charity,
another's laugh, not hers,

a sweet and cruel convulsion
of a hard creature of good fortune
that could laugh at whose expense,
a costly laugh.

The axe had fallen, the news was out,
Myrtle was coming down,
high heels clicking on the mirror stair,
wha hae with Barron's in marble hall
and panelled wall!
in my mind's eye I saw it all.

Let it come, as it will, what matter
that he, that I, that each and every one
were thrown to all that!
hang on to what you have, to that little or nothing,
the point of it all,
cling while you may to your prayer-like morning duty
daily round your beat; and visibly mark
how these things were managed
by heroes and martyrs and other poor sobbers
and creatures of the past.

2. In My Ward

Lost his job, and home in the rain.

He had been through the wringer
and he lingered about,
dangling like a loose knot.

With a trace
of the old ace in him yet,
and a wince at the pinch of the past.

A stubborn alter falter, me, dear me,
so wake up please, and be your old self again,
sitting in the noonday.

What we had all been about,
sounding along and making music:
a dip into song and you'll find me,
you'll come over, won't you,
come and see me some time?

Past the dazzle and din
to the fellow regions of the truth
of you and me and the departed,
in the third person in the past
where I'm still around and still looking
and I'll tell you what I see.

In my ward, on my beat from sea to sea,
never the sight of another,
never a human creature washed ashore,
never an earthman
to hang his hat in this air,
to dare this strand and visit me here
in his flying machine.

3. Magpies in The Sky

You can hear them in their craft on high,
in their cabins in the sky,
those lowbrow kids who fly.

I wonder how they dare,
how they go out in the chill,
playing with dangerous things,

airbound around the world,
on guard like sentinel bees
over the Presidency, over Heaven.

How tired I am nobody knows,
how I climb down the subway stairs
to the subworld, to my depths and reaches,
how my heart labors to keep on,
how heavy it pounds
to make that one next beat,
that downbeat, that fist of defiance,
and beat the rap by one more beat.

How I blow along, how I come flying
down where the train pulls in and crashes shut
to gnash its way into the leaking tunnel
and leave me standing on the stony floor
with my newspaper under my arm.

In the underground, in the stabbing light that blinds,
you read the morning news of the winter world
and those who are way up there on their rounds
when you are snug at home at rest,
settled down to a life of ease and disease,
curled into a ball, and doze away until Spring.

Wriggle in deeper into your woolly dark
and give a great yawn, and hope for the best.

No heat in my house,
the cold creeps in, the attic windows tremble,
the plaster sheds, the clapboards curl,
the wind whistles in the nail holes.

The sky is full of magpies; and for their sake
you chatter and groan: for your children in the air,
for their return, for we are surface creatures

as you saw me last, breathing hard
when the train had slammed away like a brass band
a dark and human band, a tramping horde,
a torrent a sewage of sound

And yet a mere pulse, a single knot
in that web of hour and day
through which you might trace me
if you could tag me with a luminous grain
as I tracked my way and lived my life through,
in the dark with the stabbing lights,
the local stations passing like sheet lightning
at the turn in a man's life,
as he sits reading his paper
and folds it back and tucks it under his arm.

Hints and divinations,
darkness was common to them all
and to his many narrow escapes
his lucky returns to the surface
where he found his way home

And holed up for the winter, and covered up
against those homing marauders
in the upper, outer spaces
which were like a mirror image
of the underground
reversed into a blue sky
whose bright depths were like that darkness,
its shining, its bitter mineral cold.

DOWNTOWN

1. Disaster's Kiss

Our hour is drawing to a close
and little has been said or done,
we came up with no pearl
from the dark and deep.

My name is V. I. Peep
and T.V. is my keep,
and there is no escape:
stone walls are less than air
against these voices.

Channel 3, a numbered eye,
an eye in the sky,
in sunshine and clouds and universal space,
stares you in the face and tells you:

You are fired.

The crack of doom lays bare the past
and you're in it again, back in the dark truth,
once more you know it well:

Disaster's kiss restores the sight.

2. A Market Report

And isn't that the thing to do: speak up for him?
because, you see, he was so dumb,
couldn't utter a mutter a nothing
but smash a fine old porcelain plate,
hurl a dish into the sink,
burst and curst and struck and stranded,
and undone and unbecome and gone
and forgotten it all.

And you stood up for him.

Would you stand up and say a few words?
just a few words,
a scream, a laugh your head off,
give the man a chance, let him talk,
give him his head and enough rope,
as if you cared.

And did it have to, was it really
and could such things?
and why to him, to me of all people
and why to all? a plague on all
every last one stricken
and crossed from the list and absent
in the war of man versus man
and re-enlist in the next,
and a look at the tickertape
to see if we are still in business.

A word at a time and a year at a time
I lived through it all.

In the great Crash of '29
I cracked on the Curb

because there was no yield,
unyielding and fruitless, without return,
and couldn't take it, didn't make it,
had a wife and couldn't keep her,
a forgotten and forgiven man.

Complained and reproached her
bitterly beat out a final word
and said something, but it was nothing.

Stand up for him and defend him
and stand him, how can you stand him?
slow to wrath and slow to answer,
and drive you mad.

Thirty years on the job and they'd let you go would
    they?
I'd lift the lid right off that shaft of glass and stone,
and I'd be leaning over, brimming with good humor,
a promise of better days, a raise, vacation with pay,
one big vacuation, all quiet, all out for lunch
for a have a nice week end.

I would marshall them with an arm band,
a black band
to keep them in line for one at a time
from all the exits, out with all of them
to join me and strike up the band
for the light of day,
for doing nothing in the daytime,

For outwardness,
and for you all, and for one and all,
and all for one: (me).

3. Man Wanted

So he stood in line
with his sample kit and his pitch,
and his fright when about to be heard.

Would they know him
as he slid the check through the window grille?

Look, no hands! no arms!
so couldn't possibly have forged that name,
how could he have held a pen
without hands or fingers
or any trade or skill?
stood up and hemmed and hawed
and said a few words

Even if he got by with a stolen pass
and ran for all he was worth until he fell
with a cardiac bombombardment up to his ears,
even so, he might, at that,
up and walk in with a casual air
and give his name and address,
and flash his many-colored
accordion bill-fold.

4. Beggars Around

Laboring toward the subway, your breath steaming
in the blue space, framed in a sky
of twinkling windows, high and far,
and a threat of snow

As you pushed on and fed your heart air
to reach the newsstand by the downward stair

and iron hand-rail, to descend
and vanish from the face of the earth

There you met a darkened highwayman
with gutted eyes and frost-split lip
an icicle from the nose,
and swollen hands, a rough-jaw dragger
bent at the knee
with a bareback stoop, riding the ground,
a threadbare side to the north
and a scarf loose in the freeze.

His collar up around his jaw,
and the low voice conniving in a crime,
a crime to give and a crime to take
and be taken in the crime of charity
and muttered: thanks all the same,
and god bless you and to hell with you,
can't spare a lousy coin
for a little old me-man,
you old would-be with a heart,
making a fuss about your heart,
claiming exemption, I know your kind,
a sweet guy, a dreamer,
a father, a king of beasts,
a lion hearted deerslayer,
a fellowman, a nigger lover,
a sophistical mystical wit,
a funny man.

And there was the one you took in for the night
when you were a kid reading Dostoievsky,
ashamed to be afraid to let him in
to sleep on the floor.
And the newsman by the subway stand,
his hungry five o'clock call: "All Late! All Late!"
crowing in the dusk to the homing crowd.

I haven't heard him lately, the rough-hewn little man,
his huge head and slimy eyes glaring up at you
as he palmed your nickel; a tough old dwarf,
his powerful hands sooty as a bootblack's,
buffed to a shine by the driving wind.

5. Another Beggar

My troubles are foot troubles:
never get anywhere on these feet,
flat, flat as the world is flat;
and never leave this precinct
and end up and perish in this parish.

And so you'll find him sweltering in town
like everybody, for he's only human.

A human streak, and fast, boy was he fast!
and beat the clock, and beat time,
a time beater, an egg beater, and the subject
of a famous American painting.

Sat for his portrait,
stood for election
and ran all the way home.

I wondered how he earned a living, though elderly,
his nose aflame, like a sobered up drunk,
I hate to tell this, how he stopped us on Broadway
all dressed up like Monsieur in a temps perdu,
what was he doing there, as we edged away
when he popped from the dark, and followed and
hurled that parting insult?

6. Moe Blow

Like Moe Blow
who blew in, and breathed at his desk
and never made a sound
until MacMean, the guy in charge,
started picking on him.

Well, Moe Low
just couldn't take it
from him or anybody, but he took it.

Myrtle heard his griefs at supper time
and goaded him till he was black and blue
and he took it to the front office.

So they transferred him to publicity,
but in no time something comes up,
an irritating trifle, really,
some people are just made for trouble.

You couldn't call him a trouble maker,
his resumé
was okay,
but somebody else started picking on him,
always picking on him,
like in the mean pecking order,
for he was last in line
and a poor pecker,
and that's how it was with Moe Owe,
till he was back in the front office,
and finally had to go, so he went,
and that was the last ever seen
of Moe No.

A LONG STORY

1. Their Worth Appears

Could a chance shot, a stray bullet entail such a course of
events? It was another rainy day, dragging from rain to
rain, a long train of blues and grays, weary men, mile after
mile, and none knew the colonel's orders, the cause long
lost, a leaden color pervading the countryside, where the
army tramps, the passing marksmen had left their crosses.

> The grounds overgrown with loose vines
> and clinging ivy trails,
> their tendrils ringing the dry sticks,
> clasping the stone
> in the oddest probing ways,
> hanging on and staying on,
> turning to ancience, to the patriarchal fiber
> of rocks and redwoods,
> what had withstood and remained
> of whatever falls away
> or dries up and blows away.
>
> Their frailties all put to the test,
> like the frosty flower of the alpine height,
> or the drowned sailor by the ocean treasured.
>
> Everything happened to them,
> marked and drawn,
> and weathered in the boundless past,
> until their worth appears
> to the stranger,
> to the lucky hunter on the trail,
> to the immigrant with his bundle and hunger,
> his bad cough and his watery eye.

2. Her Boy

Fict, fact, ho hum, I smell the blood of an ingle, a narrow little manch, a mere boy.

When I think of all it took to bring him to, and keep him from expiring, how she wiped out his ears and nose with little dabs of sterile cotton; and the diapers and all; and how she fed him a spoonful at a time, the leggy, smelly, fresh faced, drooly little swaddler with a waving fist, clutching a toy and baaing like a lambkin.

How, when she held a spoonful at his mouth, he agreed and opened wide and received the gift and swallowed it down, how her lips, tongue, throat, in unison swallowed with him and enacted the great big deed of a swallow it down, and once more my little wallower, my brave little swiller, one more swallow to summer it up, to supper it down, and go to sleep my bamby. How her vitals breathed with him, for she was his mother.

And so he grew and grew, and you should see him now. A good lad, and a merry young hood is he, six foot one and a half, with a low skull, crewcut, cropped to stipple and bone; bright as they come, and quick on the draw.

And she still swallows when he swallows, and pulse by pulse and word for word follows him around.

3. Courage

A hot and soggy tropical case of flight,
as far as heigho, as far as you can go
and way off and wide of the mark
for we are cowards all

who? you! me? it's only me
and my theme, Courage.

Was he a fool, just a damn fool
a foolooleroy foldefolly fool
or just a coward, a yellow fellow
a cookoo, a card
a tardy lardy lad
addled and errant as they come,
what would you say, my boy?

Say sir! say yessir! take off your cap,
your gray sombrero, lift your visor,
show us your face and smile,
that's a laddylassy, nice little dog,
look me in the eye!

That was at short-arm inspection,
when I was exceedingly shy
and the brutal barracks doctor
barked: "Face me!"
as I came up in the line of naked boys
and stooped, a little sidewise
like September Morn,
never exposed before,
never seen, my stark, my hapless self.

Courage:
guts sei dank, he had it after all.
Courage is a brave thing,
and the unlettered in Tin Pan Alley,
they wrote those songs:
The Sunny Side Of The Street
Pack Up Your Troubles,
Smile!
Smiling and Smoking Allowed.

4. Before Your Time

The whistle blew, the wretched stirred,
in their hard childhood, in their thin-clad hunger,
in the years that ring in my head,
that twirl with the yarn in the mills
to fine and finer, to spectral finest
in "the dark Satanic mills."

And the daily bread and the ovens
and how I shied away
like the iron-shod horse whose leap
struck sparks on cobblestone.

My thread is too thin, it keeps knotting
and the needle is dull from the match flame
which I use in surgery
for thorns from the garden,
for I am an expert with the needle,
I am skillful with any kind of point,
I can read the engraver's marks in a watch,
a near-sighted visionary.

Up and down the stairs
of those barn-like stores ablaze
with blinding neon signs;
manned by heavy, sour, ironic
dull boys behind the counters;
and the racked walls, the barred windows,
the grille front that folded by day,
the brass burglar sign
THESE PREMISES PATROLLED.

One night as I climbed the stair
an alarm bell went wild,
like a trolley bell in the old days,

that tore me once from sleep,
my heart hammering
to the same hell clamoring past
into the glare at the crossing

Where I lived as a boy,
between the junk castles of the El
and the turkish subway domes
of Avenues A, B and C;
up one step to a door, a hall, a cell,
a cot, a chair, a print on the pasty wall,
a false tin hearth,
and a window with the blind down.

5. Heaven Trembled

The way it was and the way it is,
the hoarse guys with a brogue
still going the same rounds
on high road and low road, making
the same sounds.

Heavy shod like those giant Brittainy steeds
with their manes way up high,
their snorts, their forelocks,
a white diamond on the forehead,
or a white band down the nose,
and the friendly brown eyes
looking straight ahead without a smile,
or the heavy head hung way down low,
such a humorless literal face,
not a spiritual, not a refined face
but a nice face.

A low soul, a horse without a spur.

Prince Henry in the saddle, a bonny prince,
up at dawn to ride and leap in English,
and a headless horseman in the Catskills
with the stars and the whippoorwill,
and the scissors umbrella man.

In the open wagon he rode his grindstone,
held an eager knife to the wheel,
it hissed and bit the stone, and a leaking cup
tinked drops of water on the whirling edge;
his face in a peacock fan, a comet tail of sparks
as he worked the treadle and made organ music.

I used to tiptoe through the great doors
and steal by hoary pillar and nave,
where I could see the distant sheaf of pipes
embossed upon the wall that arched
to a thorny gothic crown.

There, to the side, alone,
a little black-suited man
labored at the organ.

Heaven trembled and spoke
in a very deep voice.

The boy by the wing in the rear,
by the beards, by the prophets,
was lost in the sound
and dared not come out,
he might hide in a bench for a day or a year
and yet an elderly man might appear
and lift a beckoning finger
and gently motion him to leave.

6. Eye Trouble

When as a boy you put on your brand new glasses
the world sprang into sight,
as sharp as frost and stars.
And now, a white cloud ever at your side
you are concerned with vision.
A funny thing,
Moe's brother as blind as Milton
all through the war.

Always end up in war
because you see they don't agree,
just a little difference led to it all,
started from nothing at all.

Whell, hell, of course, now that you ask,
it all blanks out
suddenly he has a fit, a spell,
can't spell a little word like eye
e,y,e! oh my,
the trouble I seen,
eye trouble.

Unhappily couldn't manage it all alone; looked up a
word and it led to another and still another, a merry chase
back to the first word in the first place, and rightly so,
according to Russell, a kindred spirit of my youth, for the
best of us are tautologists all, synonomystics from way back,
and it figures after all: an i for an i, ask a wordy question,
get a wordy answer.

So what's the lowdown, what's your line? Your line is
tapped; the age of privacy is past. Notice a little peep right
in the middle of a word? It's that wire-tapping thing:

The whole town, the papers say,
is tapped twenty-four hours a day
because they want to trap Izzy Shuster
in a private chat
with his boyhood friend Lou Blue,
for his F. B. Iography

For their microphiles,
lovers of little things.

7. Sunday Morning Bell

And at the land's end the sea sparkle
where the sun slicked the pebbled beach
of green rock slime and flats of spotted shells
and shots of spray.

The sallow seabirds fell away,
their heads down and their wings high
and hung and swung
and wrung a living from the deep,
from the shallows and the island break,
the clouding and darkening.

Hid their heads under their wing
in terror of the lightning
and the thundering wave.

Tracking the sun, a red crowned Viking shell
dancing, merrily chopping forward,
leaping, cleaving the solemn sea.

Tall at the prow,
westward with the running tide,

bounding to that silence
with lightning oars.

And grounded, sprang to the sandpaper beach,
the thin pure water streaming,
racing past, seizing his armored feet.

Struck shore and planted the flag
of universal murder afoot and afloat,
and sang the anthem, God Our King.

And our choir of fellow scholars
with our wide white collars
and our preacher and our teacher,
every morning in assembly still we sang
God Our King.

In the meadow where the apples blow,
by the rutty road and the mossy
daisy dotted wayside loam
cool to our brownskin toes,
and the slippery brook
in the world-wide dawn,
our faces spring-water bright
and our sleepy eyes and blue lips,
we would start for school down the road
to the far turn over the hill
to the poor little school house.

By the square white clapboard church
with the buggy sheds weathering
on the trampled and shaded spot
by the ragged slope of graveyard slabs
with here and there through the sod
a rib or a knuckle of stone.

We never went to that church
nor stepped over that high stair,
through the double door of varnished oak.

It was for the gentiles
(with a smiling shake of the head)
of that land and that town.

The Sunday morning bell
sang pure gold,
like the sun in the sky
and the loud gold bee
and the train's faraway cry.

And once in the yard right after school,
the long legged native boy
in a leering, sneering, snotty voice,
called me a sheeny.

The class came round in a ring; I closed my eyes and saw
my father nod his big bright head, and I saw my mother's
wondering smile, as if to call me back, to run and hide
behind our apple tree, to press my forehead to the bark of
the big bellied trunk, and count to a hundred.

And be brave and step up and give him a kick in the
crotch with a heavy new shoe, and so I did, and they
howled: Unfair! kick him back! and so he did; and our
ears were soundly boxed by Mr. Hendrickson was his name.

And after we moved away, Miss Clayton sent us little
bible stories every Christmas, as if we never grew up, and
we loved her, she was no mere aimishe woman, real and
jewish, but a sort of angel like a picture in a book, made of
some sweet lamb-like thistle-blown light stuff and nonsense,
in a fine white apron or a wedding dress, like a nun or a
little dead child in a silk baby carriage, with all the won-
dering people filing by.

I saw her through the wide doors
by the stair of gilt organ pipes
in the starry interior twilight.

I saw her climb the lily-stemmed iron step
of the buggy with the high spindled wheels
and the dashboard in a swan curve
that came to a fine edge like a violin.

The patient mare's wispy mane
and long face warped like an old board
pinched to hollows at the eyes,
eyes of marble, looking nowhere;
and the leather looped to the shafts
in knots learned by a farmer's boy
when he was broken to harness
and to the hard lot
of a slim gelding boy.

The shafts of ash tapered upward
at the mare's strapped breast,
and the wheels were edged with steel
worn to a blinding flash.

How those spokes whirled,
how those rims ground and caught the road,
when the reins snapped and the mare gave stride
and the sand flew and they rolled away,
rose away into heaven,
past the turn, and into the blue.

8. Plain As Day

A slum town,
a shanty with a barber pole,
a wooden Indian
in front of the cigar store,
warping, with a dark knot hole,
as plain, as dull
as a rainwashed, peeling wall,
where the frost comes through.

There Abe made do, and wouldn't fail
when needed, when a call came through
and he sank in the powdery snow,
plodding to the holly-decked door.

Inside, a kettle singing, and everything bright
to read by firelight of tall serious men
of wit and principle, and plain as day,
true as a straight line between two points,
straight as a rip in his black coat.

Euclid's page and Noah's ark,
the due respect of mankind,
a turkey in the straw,
and take it out in tobacco,
wood, stone, water, meat,
hewn, hauled, drawn, weighed and known.

A marked man,
with a sorrowful eye when alone,
a good man with a story to warm a friend,
to cheer him on the cheerless way.

A prayerful man, in the candle glow,
with the white cloth, the sacred buttery loaf,

the china cup, and the gilt, tooled book,
the black ribbon marking the place.
All is fair, all is right on the sabbath.
Wash up, brighten up for company coming,
and shine up the brass and the silver.

Made a living in the town
and joined in song when the occasion arose
for a psalm on right and wrong,
and went along with the legend
of the Eastern star over the savage West,
the tender story of Mary and her Child,
and lent himself to ceremony,
appeared and showed himself in church,
his cracked eagle head in the doorway,
in the age of godly men
and the devil in the belfry.

9. A Short Sleep

To this lowland
of shining mist and branching stream
a cloud of thankful sprites sank to the trees,
found branch to cling and clasp, with folded wing.

They had raced the sun and the stars,
where the seas dashed high,
lifting the ship on the wave
and drowning the rockbound shore,
each rock a continent
for a pause in flight,
for rest from heaven.

And in this sanctuary the hunters found them,

their crests and wind-worn breasts,
their tight, gold-fingered feet,
their sunset colors and sunrise voices,
their dazzled, world-wide calls,
their chattering commotion
and cries from heart to heart
in the cool pine and the dark laurel
and high in a pear tree,
in the air space known to all
to be free.

Here, to the lightning and the whistling sting,
to the cracking shells of air and whips of fire
they fell and fell, in darkling fleets struck back,
in armadas of pain, they stormed the ground
and crashed to earth's embrace.

And here their plumage
was plucked and packed in sacks
for the ground-bound walkers of the field
to wear to church on Sunday morning.

And the dark banshees too in forest flight,
the traders and hunters cut them down
with all vanished beasts
and their sharp eyes and their windy hair.

10. A Past Offender

It's like the zoo or the museum, like sightseeing or slumming or why you, why not me? or a cruise around Manhattan Island on a twin screw yacht for a touraluralu through Tarahara halls or a short evening course at Ennui U., or the U. of Balabam, a Georgian studying for the priesthood, to wear a cowl, a hood who rose to power in the class war, head of his class and a good debater, a pressure boy with a little black check book in his double breasted, double dyed black overcoat.

So there's an election coming on
and who's running? why, all the boys,
all over the campus, a riot!
all out! coming through the rye,
to the arsenal, to arms!
for defense! for freedom!
for virginalia and genitalia!
to arms, the Sow is on fire!

There's a pretty girl on the campus,
on tour from Hollywood, don't miss her,
a disturbing little thing in a black skin.

She stands in her car
to the cheers and the leers,
and who threw that one? in the eye
and win a trip around the world,
a chance on the team,
and bet your bottom dollar
and last red cent
you are whiter than blacker
than browner than darker
than yellower, you lucky hound.

Marched in the Macy parade
with micky mouse,
a gunman and his moll
and Macarthur heigho,
on a flying red horse.

And the man from Missouri
with the purring catch in his voice,
like an abused and starry eyed schoolmarm
reading his speech from a large yellow pad.

With a tuneful saloonful
of barbershop balladry,
with the flag at half mast,
as the boys came marching by;
a chesty little rooster, he flew
from deck to deck, reviewed the fleet,
stood his ground at the same old stand
(a hell of a way to run a country)
and got away while he had his health,
a plain man, a common man,
a bit common but you'd love him.

Spry little banterer with a grin,
the Hero of Shima,
and none paused to wonder as he sang:
To each and all,
to every single one I tingle
with Concern & Affection.

With what awe what jubilation
you read of the star in the East,
the white man's star
that fell on Alabam, bambam!
or rather way out yonder overseas
on the other side of the world,
fell upon a multitude

and showed them what they were: dust.

Unto each and every one
what thou hast undone
with that dewdad of yours,
Sonnyboy, light of the world.

A sun shines east and a sun shines west
and I know where the sun shines best,
mahamammy! in total darkness
and in blackface, a question of race
in the race for the skies,
shattered and tattered.

And damned if he do, and damned if he didn't!
look what we done! all our own doing
all together, tarred with the same,
all of a feather, a ticklish question,
on the side of the angels, the anglomanians
who thought they won the war, hehe!
and a high diddle and a yankee doodle
and a dandy, a humdinger, that one.

It sure did beat anything in the Bible.

Zeus with his firecrackers
had nothing on Kelley up there
in his bulldozer in the sky,
and when he let go it was bigger than
what hath God wrought.

You always were a schizo,
a scratcher, an itcher and a digger,
a high flyer and a crawler
with a grand design,
two-faced and double sided,

sweet and salt and peppery, reduced to tears
when you knew those things and saw those things.

And how come you never said a word
when the going was rough
and stayed in your little back yard
while history was made? and all you did
was stand there and wring your hands.

Skedaddle while you can,
catch the next train and pay the fare,
spend it, spend it, you're not too old,
have faith, have luck, have a good time.

And why didn't you write, a line or two,
when we still remembered you?
Not even a card, and never called up,
for absence was his calling.

You have blundered out of bounds,
what are you doing here?
arrest that man! hold him in sight,
give him leave to be, to speak and be heard,
let him in, take him in.

And disposed of him, have you?
haven't seen the last of him yet,
an old turner and returner,
no known address, a past offender,
and no more room on his card.

FIVE FOOT FOUR

1. Me and Herbie

"In every shape, manner and form,"
Herbie would say, and pause
and swallow, with a lift of the jaw.

We were so alike, he and me:
point for point, in height, in collar, in hat size.

As a boy of seventeen
I shrank from putting on the white smock
of a short order waiter.

When I saw him behind the counter,
him and Pop, both in white, side by side,
in the uniform of servitude,
how I backed away!
I would not wear the white habit,
crisp as a nurse's or a nun's,
soon greased with bloody smears,
I shuddered at that shroud,
yet there they were, my own, my nearest,
ranged with the enemy, and God was with them
and the odds against me.

I thought I'd manage,
flatfoot on the sidewalks hot and cold,
and cover ground, come what may,
on my night watch, doing time,
but I was no good in a winter drizzle,
with a bad left side,

a poor head and a lame arm, what a man,
what a veteran,
what a sign of the times
for a feature in the Sunday paper.

A southpaw, a wag and a dog,
an ugly mugly,
like my neighbor who, the papers say,
is away on a five year rap;
he too imagines himself
a comrade of the immortals,
holding forth behind the bars,
venerably joking
with his boon self-celebrants
at his ninetieth birthday party
in Valhalla or somewhere,
wherever he went.

2. The Lost Word

A little mixed up, like Emma
with a story in her smile, in her eyes,
gazing toward a ceiling in the sky,
and the thread of the story,
somehow the curl of the tale with a twist
is lost in a smiling cloud,
and she cries: No! and starts again,
and who knows the story?
and comes to me,
a match in one hand and a needle in the other,
always gathering thorns in the garden,
and I must take them out, one at a time.

I can't remember, I am so tired,

no violence please,
temerity and dexterity, yes,
and that other something, what was it,
a notion that caused a commotion
and dazzled a generation of teachers
and young book reviewers
of the charm school of critischism.

Austerity?
The jewel of a thought is gone.

So we'll do without, we're good at that,
and we'll get along, never mind.

Decorum, the lost word!

I'm all for decorum. I recall with discomfort
my uncouth behavior toward practically everybody,
and I must and I will, yes, one of these days
I'll go to each and every one
and explain and expire.

3. Jamus Died

You could swear he was alive
his cold cheek shining and his hard eye bright
as he lay in the strength of his flesh and bone
as if, just as if alive,
a stranger in a box, a something strange
moving away from here through the door
in formal attire.

Yes,
now's your time to confess.

Why were you late,
too late for love, too poor to love
in this city of diamond dust
where Jamus died,
wrong, deep in wrong, living in wrong?

What's done is dung, can't be undone
so come to yourself
and show a little forgiveness,
for if you have not charity?

And bejesus, why was this masochrist
punishing himself,
driving himself to work, forever in arrears?

Surely he had paid enough, done enough time
and wasted enough, so why not let him off,
give him a white pill and send him away
to compose himself for sleep.

4. Arthritis

A bad time, being dreamed through by this terrible
dream. For instance, one of the girls noticed you holding
your hurting right hand, and you thought or said something
witty about the weather and your arth rightis handis. Well,
anyway it hurt something awful.

(The gas station man had knotted hands like a leper;
they were purple in the frozen air; he couldn't turn the
screwcap of the tank in my car. He died that winter.)

In the crowd, by the grandstand, on a bench in the park,
this girl said something, a word of advice I think, with
reference to my painful hand; it seems to go way back,

when on my way to school I squeezed my arm through the
white picket fence, and couldn't pull my arm free, and
wouldn't let go the flowers; we'll have to censor this no
doubt. And then of course, the ticket window on the Ele-
vated, and the kids sneaking by, and the ticket chopper,
he saw them, and caught my eye as I was passing through,
out into the park, to wait for the northbound train, where
I took a plush seat with a high back.

>It was night time and too dark to see
>Flora's golden head,
>her honey hair brushed and braided tight;
>in a tearful way you knew her to be there
>and felt her there, your heart complaining.

>The spaced, paced music pulsing bar by bar,
>like a faraway, marching heart,
>a solemn breathing, from beat to beat,
>drummed itself out of itself,
>trembled itself out
>through the leaves of the trees
>on the concert lawn in the park.

>It all came from this painful golden arm,
>it went back to this stretch of pain,
>to where I left my brief case
>on the shadowed lawn
>under the stars, behind the tall iron gate,
>and went to find Flora, over there in the crowd,
>still on the move, looking for Flora,
>I was trying to tell her,
>right here, I think, right where
>there was no hide nor hair
>of my cowhide briefcase

I looked high and low, in the aisle and on the benches,
and under the seat in the train, on the floor and in the grass

on the lawn. No brief case and I would kill myself yes and so I would, and that was what I would have to do, now there was nothing to do but that, the only thing to do, and that was that. I knew it, and I knew it all along the thing to do, and in fact that was what I was telling Flora, though she was not listening.

> I was breathing
> that pulsing, beating
> burden of my music, my woe,
> and sobbing it out in time,
> sobbing myself away,
> it was a dream, and my brief case,
> let's see, my leather brief case was not really
> lost
> and where in the dawn haze
> in where were we?
> and there it was! my testament,
> the pages grayed over by the wooly whorls
> of my golden hand,
> my gambling hand that rolled out
> my words of chance, read 'em and weep.

> A dime a dozen
> or a penny a hundred, or give 'em away,
> or find a taker, if you could,
> a junken driver to pick 'em up,
> for what? what for?

> My psychic hand, my knowing hand is in pain,
> and doesn't want to,
> the moving hand that writes on the wall
> has changed its mind
> and won't go on,
> a painful choice
> and hurts me more than you.

MEMORIALS

1. Maxwell: Down He Went

Fresh from the market, revived in the wash tub, in the
    blue crystal
water, the wide-awake, water-bright carp, in a gracious
    turnabout,
a sweep of the tail and a stately tour of the tub.

As clear-cold as the jellied fish transparent on the
    table dish,
laid out on the porcelain platter, with the fine linen
    and the silver,
the sterling character lying there in profile. And I
    knew it, I knew
we'd touch on that party again, it would surface and
    surprise us,
on our feet again and cold sober.

A cardiac case was brought in, thrashing on the
    stretcher,
and heaved and struggled for air.

A dead fish in a slum, alleyoop!
the kingpin, they knocked him down,
saint though he was and immortal,
with a cold fish eye on occasion.

As if through a glassy aquarium wall
I see the East Side shore becalmed
and the hospital cot where he lay,
in the seasick bedside air,
the man who was killed.

Down he went in a stink by the slimy curb
in the dark of the narrows
in the alley where he sank
and went under.

Where he shuddered and choked,
the white moby, the dicky white
white man, Macmanx the cat walker
from the South, from the deep deep,
a real cat from all the way back,
from the wide wide wake, the big fish story
of the giant fibbibia, the ailing South,
the raging Souwouth is where he was from,
Saint of the lees of the south'n blooze,
a boozer, a whoosier from Natchez.

A handful,
the nine or the twelve, how many were they,
followed him around, on a sabbatical
from a small university town, for a thesis
on the tale of this tom in a tub.
Rubba hubba, they rubbed him out
and so he made the headlines all over page one
and fame was his at last.

(When the dawn found them, if you could see
how his little boy
sat on a cot and cried and brooded.)

Yeh, I knew him and outlived him,
and what's all dis about de nouth and de south
and where there was a war on,
and where were you then?

Why, I was a veteran
of the previous war.

Of the waswar of the wahren
for the warheit and freiheit
and the light of day
in warzeit.

The world was coming round
to honor that fond maniac.
The bell rang
and out in the hallway a bevy of men
of my race and time.

Into my funeral parlor, said the fly,
come in, gentlemen!

They wanted to be in the act, to touch him,
the Kilroy who never was there,
so they came to the home of this guy
who had known him when young
and green and cold.

Out there in the coldwater flats
like low tide in Seagate
where the rocks and the gulls gave you the shivers.

And why I dwell on that I don't know,
a matter of where you find yourself,
and willynilly go on from there
and keep going, never better.

2. Myrtle, A Mourner

The seated women looking at Myrtle,
a handkerchief overflowing from a tight hand,
her spent smile, fragile in her tears,
in mourning she was best
and all was best and for the best.

And I thought of that word again: decorum,
and interior decoration.

They came and went, and paid their mite
to the dark widow in her gown of darkness.

Strange as it seemed, you were there,
an odd sight
for a painter of another age,
as you sat in the straight-backed chair,
a character in silhouette,
in that sanctum of mortality,
all surface to the artist's eye,
a light and a shade and a cast,
a name, a numeral, as he rendered you
and made you, a cryptic, pigmented
seated sarcoph, a Gus
in a time and place,
in black and white
in pale antique etch
in cuneiform
in Assyrian sandstone
in square cut marble,
in an unuttered sound,
dear Lore, in a tear.

And not so bad after all,
not quite like those other funerals
which had been so difficult
and blinding and hard on the eyes.

TO COME TO LIGHT

1. What If So?

If you ever turned up in those haunts
past the thicket of wild roses,
the thorny clusters and braided vines,
and entered once again, if only once,
the inviolable place,
though such entering were a crime,
and were locked away, the invisible man,
a prisoner asleep on his cot,
the small barred window high out of reach,
where one might never see
a little wilde cloud
melting in the blue?

In an iron mask,
with a slit for an eye;
around his neck a golden locket and chain,
a martyr
of the sun's halo round her hair.

And what if so, what if we were concerned
with his conviction,
his awakening and his need
of seeing how it was
and what became of him
and what would become of us,
how it was all transmuted and muted
and never came to light?

What if words failed you,
those other words unsaid and never sent?

2. In That Age

Fact! the ring of the truth
in my native land, in the morning paper,
and there you have me, brother,
my old eyes ringed with treble trouble.

He wears no crown, no leaf, no thorn,
but the mere weight of his years;
he is tired,
a ward of the A.S.P.C.A.,
the kindly souls who find you
when you fall by the wayside
as darkness comes over you,
and the devil take you,
or the department of sanitation.

The view from the solarium:
the roofs and the streets of parked cars
cradling the city dust as the snow hardens
to a darkening crust
strained from the city air.

There the cailer at the door will find him,
in that age, among those portents,
in that race, that maze,
that vast past and present place
marked by tombs and flags and flashing signs
and thunder on wings, there he stands in sight
and turns and walks off down the way,
to be enfolded in absence, in the lux
of the unknown nature of things.

And in due time it will arrive,
a phone call,
credible and human, cool with news
from the unexplored, the boundless outer West,
calling the young away.

3. If I Could

Locked away in a damp house
in a hiding place, unsafe in the safe,
in the darkness of the race.

Like those two brothers who tunneled about
and passed out among their effects
and the secret was out, out for an airing
in the morning paper, in a funnysheet,
like a map, a vast plain, a countryside
which you spread out to read
over the gleaming kitchen floor.

If the past could say a few words
if under ether, or in the oven fumes
I caught my breath
at a man aflame, the fiery cast
of all thou hast of the past

As if I knew the way
and had my way and sang
and said a few words

As if I were a Whitehead,
with a good head and a sound head,
a poor dumb browbeat
honeybuzzed arrowing bonehead,

headed for the boneyard
where I picked up the skull of a horse,
the hollow eyed, saw-tooth jawbane
of Mister Ichthyosorrio,
an immigrant farmer gone West,
a young man in a checkered vest,
a stone man, a sage,
a bushman of the trackless past.

Came into the world
without a scrap or a stitch,
arrived penniless and whole,
empty handed and sound of limb,
raring to go, where and what for?

I'll tell you what for and I'll give you what for,
and you'll know or you'll think you know.

Isn't it outrageous for a cracked, sacked, conceited little
        grinner
to go and print a collection, crammed with the letters of his
        betters
and stick himself right in the middle, and get away with it?
He did, and he put his friends in, here a friend and there a
        friend
and me in there too, another one of those, I suppose,
a disgrace to his race to show his face among the immortals.

Another load for the archives,
good for the fire hazard.

Is it too much to ask?
a little something, a solid gold ring, a blue diamond,
a week-end pass, a holiday look around,
and take tea and break bread
with a noble kinsman's child?

And must it be so? for a man has a gift,
as the snake his fang and the jewel in his head,
and the cat his retractable claw.

While beings of the field may sleep,
he must beat out his time
through webs of leaping spindles, throbbing looms,
a weaver and a griever.

The sage of old never heard
the clapping shuttles in the Satanic mills,
nor was Plato concerned
with prisoner and slave.

4. A Worldly Man

Play ball! The southpaw on the mound
joins his hands as if in prayer,
and then forward, a giant stride,
the invisible ball goes crack!
and history is made.

Time to play ball
but he didn't show up on the lot,
a lame arm and a bad eye;
repaired to his study to think things through,
till the season and reason had fled.

Willingly would he forego
and gladly resign if he could and let go.
but he is strong, his heart beats steady
and he tips the scales at 170,
thirty pounds over his fighting form.

And it's daylight again:
the world's face clears, the sun breaks through,
and I wonder where I've been.

5. The Truth

So we've settled down
on our bed of nails, our nettlenest,
our viper in our shirt of hairy breast,
and a sighing, a lying in his heart,
and on his back at last, and come to rest.

Oh what a gee wot a way
to get you out of yourself
to see yourself like thisthat.

Deal yourself out,
pass yourself out, a playbill
to tell the world.

If I wrote with the speed of electrons
electing and detecting,
making history,
for scholars in a commotion,
who would read it all? for it would be in code.

The precise truth,
what Whitey the old smart-head called it:
a fake, or more charitably, a mistake
of the errorists,
the merry old careerists
doing business with reality.

A disconcerting, baffling, paradoxy contradiction
of the tird, fourt and fift law of thermomimics, hot
          antics,
the infinite reality copied out, and none the wiser,
and all that expended energy, where did it go,
and who asked you, and who is this answering?

6. In The Same Line

Herbie's boy couldn't sleep.
bewildered by Shelley and Jesus.
And what would become of his little girl
with the great big serious eyes,
her blond hair parted tight,
a ribbon braided in, ending in two bows,
down the sharp little shoulders?

Give her a big hug and set her down
to run off out of sight.

The shaven-head priest with rimless glasses
talks so matter of fact
of birth and burial, prayer and despair,
and looks grief in the face,
worn by his tasks
to sublime care,
while I am merely tender hearted,
elderly, prone to tears,
with a tremorous knee.

Though we are in the same line: mankind,
going up and down in the world.

SHOW BUSINESS

1. At Gull's Gallery

And the high point of the evening:
you rascal you, you old adman, oh you!
caught by the young thing she was,
with wide awake midnight eyes,
staring right at you.

Held his breath, gazing back at her,
how straight she stood,
a proud, high breasted child,
do not frighten her away
as she confesses in her singing voice
fresh as grape on the vine,
her faith in Mr. Gull's
Unity of Opposites, The Key To Art.

As her eyes grew nearer and deeper still,
as she decided on defiance
and let her anger show and turned away
with dazzling head held high.

Had a lovely chat, and
pearls before girls.

Here was an old genius
with a pocketful of gems,
every one an imie,
and they dared not take them,
went into shock when I laughed at the notion
of Dürer in such a game with Saint Sebastian
who, unlike the speaker of the evening,

had never heard
of that bat from their master's head
on the apples of Cézanne.

2. In The Act

She stood in the chorus line
and kinked a knee and sang a ditty,
as Groucho twitched his great big eyebrow,
and his baritone rang out across the snow
as he tipped his big segar
and sneaked up to Mary.

And in a twink she covered up
in her mink, cool and cute,
with her dimple and her cheek,
singing of daddy in Texas.

Showed her teeth, and exit in the wings,
and back in thirty years to take a bow
as little Peewee, Peter Pan,
what a player, what a tart
bless her elfin little heart.

Out in the cold, under the lights, she sang:
All Alone in The Arctic Zone.

In the new ice age, the era of freezers.
Heaven preserved us and kept us fresh,
T.V. was our society,
our heaven and our salivation.

May all your wishes, dreaming
of a white Christmas,

may all your chrismisses
may all your mistresses
be white,
and black and tan and true.

Some showgirl!
not a literary homogeny maledictory boy
but a girl, a bee-winged honey
with her smooth white longleggy prance
for daddy.

He of the poisoned ear,
the kingly ear deafened by death,
destined to die by ear,
by the whisper of the kingly fate,
to lose a throne in pentameter.
Fetch me a mirror
and speak to it the immortal lines
through the teeth and the resonant sinus,
through the skull of the evil mind
of heaven's duality, the trembling theme,
male and female and the destined fall,
how a mime could tower like that,
descend the stair like Isadora,
to a love seat elegantly carved,
a Chopin crescendo,
applause and laughter.

So you see what a girl can do to a man,
when Mary Martin clings or wings into song,
and that was what they wanted,
to prove that this showgirl could act,
could cry, could die, knocked about like a star,
flying and falling, like all earthly things,
spinning closer, ever closer,
to come here, and here lie, and be near.

3. Danny Does It

When our Danny hurries in, hold your breath,
he'll split that second and ride that high cycle
with no hands.

A mere lad with bony knees
and empty pockets and nothing up his sleeve,
nothing but his stringy white arm,
he flies in on his bike, and he's high,
a starlike fever in his eye.

Our Dannybird, king of storks,
wings out in a high step
and you know him instantly, your long lost
crazy wandering boy blue, come back
you big boy of bloody royal hue.

What do you think of my frostbitten
tousled redhead in his open shirt,
on the brink of the stage, and what
do you think of him now,
stopped cold on the edge of the void,
the sea of eyes,
the night world looking up,
as he comes forward
to a stop before you leap,
and clasps his hands
as if flirting with death or something,
with that same lurking smile
that will drive you mad.

Actually this young jinx, this charlie chap
is a wit from other days,
a corker from a cockney bar, a bummer
from the pages of the legendary bards,

a thing of tatters,
with his secret wealth and his stealth
and his devious glance,
warming up to a song and dance
to rattle his frozen bones

And out comes an easy roar
a big voice, a loving voice
for he knows you well,
and I bet you he'll get you
with a side-kick from the knee,
a grace note, a catch in the throat,
and a laugh and a half.

4. Had To Come Out

I had to come out
and I came out, dark all over.

I was an inkspot, you know,
an india inka, one of that famous quintet,
the pinka spinks, a spunky little band,
plucked our way from town to town,
played our ringy verses
from Nixeyland, from de land of notten.

Like Colonel Jerry or Saint Jerome
or Jerry Kern or Cohn
who coined a tune or two,
Canny Day, another nightbird,
Dinney the Ginney,
my old timers and grimy rhymers
with our wings and fiddle strings
and rhythm in our wishbones,
our hip bones, our shinbones, our shining bones
rolling along, along the wrongtime.

With kerchief under chin
and nothing else but
wrack in our marrow.

Had to grow old and darken
and blacken in the bracken.

And how do you feel
about them blackbirds over there
by themselves?

Oh, there? It is bitter out there.

Ask a foolish question
and pay no attention.

Thanks for letting me in,
a minor pot, black as a kettle,
a bright darky ting aling,
way down, irking in the shadows,
a long way from home.

It's how you feel, if you do feel,
towards your wards
and from all harm,
like your little tommy tiger
dozing on the rug
with his paws tucked under.

For it's me, oh lord,
me, just as I am, and still am,
I flew all the way South
and flew back Nouth again
on the wing of that there plane,
flew from the States back to the States,
where they loves the folks they hates.

OUT AND AROUND

1. Another Chance

Said Heraclitus:
the life of fire is the death of air
and the life of water is the death of fire.
With Socrates,
all turns elsewhere, sphere within sphere,
in an astronomy of soul.
And then Jesus, an outsider,
"a nuisance in the synagogue,
citing lilies and fishes,
not in discourse, not to observe
but to declare and command,
a lordly schizoid and a foreigner,
an insufferable intruder."

They died bearded youths
gray and gone in their prime.

And what did the Frenchman,
looking at the ever staring clock
clacking its tongue at you, clear as day,
what did the frenchy say, the rhyming monk,
looking up he said: it is time to be drunk.

Heraclitus with a clockwise face
scolded the dionysiacs and damned the poets,
he was all for a universal dryness and brightness
versus wetness,
and they still call him The Obscure.

Imagine him and Mr. D. H. Lawrence
the dark boy from the underground,
face to face in Mr. Auden's anthology.

Who will judge them,
their signs and stumblings in the mother tongue
of archaic man and future man,
the gone and the quick, kin of tomorrow,
and know them through and through
in plain English, with ageless wit,
with charity to my old friends,
my poor relations and all-time losers
who died without a second chance?

2. Surprise

In the face of the truth he blew
the bazookas of his calling.

Eaten up with ambition and hate,
living off the herd,
tending and shearing the public domain.

No warning sign to the skids, and you're out!
and now where are you?

Above the clouds, the ghost plains,
the white herds of the past.

A little human dog in a tin wing
a tissue paper kite
blown away without a string,
without a silver cord
from the belly earth below
through a yawning age
to a standstill in the sky,

Awake, reborn, a diamond in the sky,
a snowflake in a scheme of ice and light

Climbed out of sight,
a thing with a sooty wing,
leaning on space,
a fixed star, a turning crystal
past choice and death.

Oh, naked earth, please let me down
and whirl me to sleep like one of those
who never rose from such a sea,
when we only dreamed of flight!
back to that humble time,
with Jesus and Heraclitus,
my fellows and friends,
to walk and talk of hearth or fire.
I came up just for the ride,
for a look and a guess
at our lands of the air
and the world's bright end.

3. Out And Around

He is down, like a pocked meteor
a cold head lying on its side
a slab on the sands.

When called upon to rise
this Odessian from the Black Sea
reached out, fumbled and muttered,
a difficult, confused old man.

A mine-dark Yorkman, a black from below,
inaudible, misunderstood.

As gentle Will wrote on his tomb:

No digging! Bones and curses!
What have we of the man Moses,
or Leonardo with all his notes in backhand?

What drove him from book to book?
It was that way with him, this way and that,
a near thing,
booked as a vagrant,
no sign of the ship he came on,
in what year, from what port,
over the border or under the rainbow,
no pedigree or warrant, and couldn't hold him,
it didn't matter, he was not wanted.

All his works remaindered
from Spring lists and Autumn lists
to a sad reckoning
in the open air, in the fog, tabled
with the bargain books on their backs,
all turning one color, under one flag:
a price tag on a stick.

As for his story,
a job for the reader of all he had borne,
to do him justice; a man like Mr. Faulkner:
to know him through and through,
rage and forgive and deliver him,
herculean and only half mortal,
begotten, bedevilled, belabored, and lived.

When he reads to you
in his soft treading monotone,
singing you the everflowing story,
then you know it through and through,
you are dreamed out and awake,
he had reached you in time, a friend,
speaking of men and of you.

4. Overdue

You know how it is,
the cold look and the silence:
Overdue.

Couldn't we get an adjournment
bail and a getaway
or a fellowship for another year or two
or three for posterity?

A case of books, inside and out,
a doctrine of tales, a tale of doctrines,
a matter of business, a business of being,
a mortal solo.

They had a way of speaking in quotes
and smiling their way to the close
of a closed question
but I got away, I couldn't stay.

And now, what can you say, what do you see?

A dadali landscape, bright as day
and silent as the dead.

No news, no word of Moe
the all-fired enthusiast
who lost heart and missed a beat
and is missing and overdue.

THE OUTER LAND

Dust On Spring Street

1

The floor boards have a sour breath
Cadaver lips apart,
The ribbed planks, furred with dust
Smell like a beast in the zoo.

This moulting back of the world
Swarms to the nostrils,
A harsh cellar mould,
Or marsh's smoky dew,
Hoarding the droppings of the air,
Ashes of insect wings
And strands of human hair.

Jeweled with the world's wealth,
With powdered mica, coal and stone,
A dust to mine, a dust of treasures,
A matted mountainside,
Its darkness inhabited
By wonders of creation and decay,
Yawning in the season of warmth,
A sea, brewing its own seed.

Inhuman dust,
It will outwait the planet's night,
Freezing tight to an acid shell,
Lie in the arctic pall,
Ice-tooth bared to the winter,
Sleep where the dark is, and come to life,

And there, god help him, if a man go lost,
He is burned by the secret touch
And suddenly athirst.

Fevers the air with fireflies, flying nettles,
Enters his eyelids and his hair,
Rises in a dream of alarm
To do him harm.

The dust arrived,
Weathered the years afar,
Traveled on the fronts of rain,
The cloudburst and the forest crackle
And desert storm,
The blind migrating host
Sailing like flocks of birds,
Ashes from the prairie burning
And diamonds from the mountain flame
And atoms riding from the stars,
The airborn offal of the fog,
The coral salt and crumbled rock
Ground to all logic's end,
Silent as the reason spent,
As pollen lost and locust fallen,
And then from darkest fold
And earth-pore, as the wave unfurls,
Smouldering in its self-born fire.

Oh, what a dust is this,
A dust both living and dead!
It was the desert bread
On which the martyrs fed.
Now in this dust a naked youth
Stands wondering,
How had he come,
How had he blundered here?

2

Between the cold plaster walls
Where the old beams breathed,
Slow with the mystery of the rite,
In mourning through the winter and the spring,
He washed the floor down to its sour flesh,
Ripped the dry crust, scrubbed with alkalis,
And fought the dust with paint and brush.
But always the snarl was there,
And every day it mocked his door.

Here was the enemy, the seeded air,
Omen of storm,
The first gray flake upon the lip.

Here the dust lived,
In this warped, crumbling house.
He dug a penny, 1904
Under the rotting leaves
Of newsprint and linoleum,
Green-minted from a mossy seam
Where the roaches come to life
And move into the night behind the beam
To sleep for ages more.

How one may share these walls
With the terror-stricken mouse,
How in this architecture sleep and rise,
None, none can tell.
None, how he disappeared,
The hapless youth in a forgotten war,
So far away, no message could be sent,
No map, no story and no word of glory,
As once it was behind a wall in Rome
And in the London alley.

The house of dust still stands,
A lad lives on the second floor.
Go through the night and climb the groping stair,
And you will find him there, wondering who you are,
Saying a shy *come in.*

The landlord comes,
The place is sold, and will be sold again,
The grime will gather on the sill,
The stair will hold until the wreckers come,
The walls will groan, the story will unfold:
Make of it what you will.

3

You have seen the dust
In solar span, the angel at the gate,
Your demon and your child, the face your own,
Yourself the enemy in fear of man.

Now if you can,
Oh, look again and see the end.
And let your blundered heart
Die in that rain, erase
The face confessed and damned.

However long, however late,
Then grieve and wait
Until the wounded air
No more offend.
And hope not to atone,
And seek not to defend:
But if you will,
And by your soul intend,

Then rise, then dare,
Defy the ashen fiend,
He trembles to the end.

Fear not the man of hell,
And seize his fiery hand.

Hymn To Logic

When your skill is dead
it is the aimless spar, and the rock diminishing
in the sea's insistence,
and it is the sea giving way,
dispersed and vapored into every being's pore,
it is any and all forms of yielding,
of falling asleep, of passing from the day.

Absence is the key,
absence, the ended toll of the bell
that swims to the heart,
disputed and pronounced
a lesson in vista,
in that tending and attending
which is as narrow as the fan of sight
and as various as the light.

Man, swarming like the water,
as fierce, as wary and as weak,
visible in the word
and scheming salvation by the word,
weighs the meaning by the meaning,
the living and the dying
that enters like the dew
the air to which I am drawn
in the journeys of all being,

in the sounding and the trying,
in turn the prey, the flesh, the excrement,
the soul in brittle age,
and the bright sand,

And in the toils of the design
the whole dark span is mine
(my breath your word
my soul your sign).

To this transparence man is born
and walks the wave: this sea is home.

To Live In Sound

1

In images of love the music shines.
It is the bird in hidden nest,
The bright eyed beauty, heart to leaf,
Quiet in paradise.

It has the thunder and the mountain calm
and wandered sea,
To chorus in its reason.

Distance strikes the chord
Vista sings the word,
And raises music's wing.

Solemn is the hero's might
To part this desert sea,
To walk the fateful ground,
The life and death in sound.

2

Beethoven! to your icy brow
My prayer was whispered low.

Here once you heard me weep,
Gave me your tender hand
And led me to this land.

Now in the universal sky
Our star new found
Moves beyond the night,
And though in ashen rain
The world were strewn,
Returns, completes the round
And blazes into noon.

Oh, hercules of love,
Dark head, corona maned,
We too in wonder turn,
In thanks resound.

High is the chord and free,
The sphere unbound,
The choir of humankind.
Thanks to the hero's might
Who thunders in this heaven.
Thanks that the soul arrived
And named this continent
And the deed of light
Is thus rewarded
And in creation's breast
Is so recorded.

In The Poor Light

1

I think of that burdened man
who seems always about to cry out
to strike the air to no avail
and I remember my own hard times in my youth
and see myself old
hoarding a dollar bill against the last day
against the cold, the only thing I fear,
the ever-shrinking cold,
the waiting the delaying the evil complying,
waiting perhaps for Spring,
standing on a deserted station
to flag a train that will never arrive,
never come crowing from the horizon,
never come ringing, never the high striding train
sliding to a stop by the frozen siding.

And the cold in the decaying house,
the uneasy rafters, the spreading seams
the thawing mire
the perpetual winds nowhere at rest
the long blasts of bad news.

Let the voice be cracked and unendearing
but no more to deny, no more to comply,
and make clear how we have come,
how we have blundered in the poor light,
the tireless eye still mine,
and my aging brothers
in the same evil pass.

2

Oh, friendless poetry,
can this fallen man be you,
this stray dog
whose pillow is the curbstone?

Heir of neglected monuments,
mayor of the littered alleyway,
dean of so be it,
master of go your way,
of the numbed fist, the frozen eyelid,
the cracked lip tempered to the wind.

You are the one,
and it is Wantless Day in Undone City
celebrating the hand withheld
the eye unanswered
the censored word deleted, charmed away,
the crime allowed, disclaimed
unlit, unshamed,
the debt deferred, the gain devised
the level eyed impunity
the hardy will engaged
deep in the predicament,
keeping the keys, serving the balance sheets.

The good sighers and the brave denyers
the quiet liars loyal to their own,
pressed between the mortgage and the deed
the word and the bond,
here ours, and all else queried, crossed from the list
with a flourish in the signature.

In the wind nowhere at rest,
in the poor light I see them, unforgiven.

Genus Wordberry

If this should be my way,
To scratch the bleak paper field,
Live by the season's chance
And tend this garden, mine until I fail,
Who would refuse my tart wordberries?
In the dark cluster, stem and thorn,
A heady distillation.

If you know how to read,
You will see a face plain as a flag,
It will tell its names and ages
And the lands of its birth,
In the cipher of its heart,
A key to all interiors,
A script for actors, histories,
And spaces folded like closed books.

By the good fortune of the season,
This wet-browed berry from my garden
Has a radiance answering back, a brightening gaze,
A secret burning look,
Rosy-skinned, hunger bearing,
Like a child's cheek aflame

Quenching and teasing still,
Urging the thirst anew,
Full as the hurrying spring
Singing: more, take more,
You can never take enough,
There is more, still more, without rest,
The heart quicker, demanding more,
Singing: come nearer, nearer still,
The crowded breath answering:
More, echoing, more.

Memorial

To my Mother, Rachel, 1876-1946

1

Wronged, wronged by all.
When you called I did not hear.
And none was there to see you fall,
Eyes round, and the wing mired,
And no one near.

Here is your print, a yellow leaf
Burning away into motes of the air,
Rising in a shaft of light
In universal dark and sand,
A trace in the sea of air,
No longer yours or mine
Or past or yet to come,
A wingflit in the wooded night
Of the whole forest in its might and mould
And leaf vein and the spider's hair
In the moon glare.

So too I seek you in my mother tongue
Until I hear the tinkle of joy
Arrayed in your smile.
And on the octave it resounds,
The blare of grief in the breast.
Then I behold the dark untold
And the wrong done, the wrong,
The sparrow falling.

2

What is it I have known,
As to the dark I sigh?
Ah, children of the world,
You are the heaven
To which I die.

Some words are found in jest
And some from joy are pressed
And some spring like the tear
Afire in the eye.
But when the word for death is born,
Then all stand in a swoon
As in a gale.

When the silent woe is ripe
In fruit to fall,
It is then the private death
Becomes the funeral,
And the one darkly struck down
Is visible to all.

I see her lowered into the raw ground,
a little man reading rapidly from a book,
the ruddy digger's boot on the blade
striking the wet sand
and the first spadeful rattles down
where she is struck again,
sealed in the insult, stoned to the end.

And we who stood and moaned,
we made no outcry, dared not stir,
a little host unarmed and wounded blind.

The whiteness of the moth and of marble
when she is helped, propped up to breathe,

her old arms, labor drawn, across the sheet
and the speckled hands of age,
seen now in farewell,
saying no, no, crying out no,
how can such things be,
in endless yielding borne,
and in the last look told.

The hidden plaint, the tender pain
the friendly, unregarded pain,
the old laundered linen face
seeking you in so soft a way
to know if all were well.

I can no longer see her face
and I do not know how it may be found
by a whim of the lost time,
it is there, with my love, her dear estate,
her sky, her birds, her lawn, her vase of flowers,
all wept away to the heart's hidden land
the land of those lost to the sight

Vision's creatures that we are,
strays of the light.

Fear Thou Not

Fear thou not the heat of the sun,
The burning sun is kind,
The blundering friend
Though he burn you blind.
Keeps his distance in the sky,
Healing, blooming in the end.
But beware thy secret eye
Mirrored in thy brother's mind.

Tiger, tiger, burning bright,
When you find your lair at night,
Press your kitten to your breast,
Nurse the angel in your nest.

Fearful is the light
That prowls the forest green:
The beast steals on unheard,
The eye burns on unseen.
Soon, soon, the skies will part,
The light will rage afar,
The earth will be a star.

To Be

1

To be the one,
The one who is afraid,
Who is shamed, betrayed,
To give one's name, to wear the yellow star,
To be in the trap, in dread of all,
And take the total evil to the end,
And know that fearful man
Can do no more to man,
And fear no more.

2

To be forgotten and forget,
And seek and fail.
Come, take the subway home,
Climbing to the dark street,

Walk house to house, each one the same,
A hidden number on the door,
Your own, then not your own.
Where do you live? In a secret nest,
There in a bright walled room a golden head
Dreams on the snowy pillow, dreams of you,
And on the door there is a lock to your key:
Where is the key and where the door?
How had you strayed, how will you guess,
Who will scan your face and tell?

3

To be and not to be:
The relic treasured, encased in glass,
Oneself inferred therefrom
By a dactyl and a black molar,
To gleam and seem.

And to be yielding, soft, alluvial,
The melting eye, the web that holds the light,
The flowered ear, the tender fingertip,
The heart's nest, close and warm,
The lip that smiles in sleep
And with the sunturned petal weakens, falls
With all that falls away,
Leaving no sign, no shell:

A secret in the air
That parted once and closed
And moved away.

Moon

How wide the wakeful eye,
How clear the night
In onward sweep.

I held this light in doubt,
Yet now it does arrive,
It does appear.

The earth and bone
To this salvation dies,
And knows the moon's white smile.

And well I know
This scarred and cratered face
On me forever bent.

The quiet conqueror,
She comes in peace
And where she comes is queen

And spends her grace,
And here resumes her right
Smiles on the sun's decline

And walks her region vast,
And stands in her domain,
The chasms of the past

The travelled soul's design.

The Notebook

To Samuel Greenberg

You shy boy standing there alone
shamed by the drowsy eye and the slow tongue,
you with blue-cold shanks in the stained trousers.

You nursed your body's need, a sweaty child,
you sat on the park bench in the glassy morning
where the skeletal city was revealed.

You pedalled through day after day on the sewing
   machine
under a yellow light in a room heaped with rags,
and labored at your verses in the notebook
which you carried in your shiny jacket
like a wad of thousand dollar bills.
Then from the bed in the public ward
you wrote a postcard to your friend the poet
and left your clothes to be burned.

You learned the new-born words
that froze to the stern morning,
the icy cobbled sky,
you nursed yourself on the spartan promises
of the night half of the world
and your book was swept under a dark stair.

Your bones complained and every plague of the time
was in your hasty birdbreast breathing.
With the ghetto fly you drowsed and fell
from the fortitude of the tender eye
and of the whole race of man
suffering the worst of the oblivious land,
foundering where the ship turned
and steamed away.

From the undulant wharf
you were blown toward the city winter
with one change of underwear, one pair of socks
and pad and pencil, your erring compass
to take your bearings by the heavenly word,
and there it was that you of all men
wrote the spacious parable
in the yellowing notebook, in the pencilled trace
sharp as the veins in the failing leaf
in each same wafer of the innumerable host
that rides the cold blast,
travels the whole sky and reaches the earth
and in the end nestles in a rocky nook
and there endures another birth
in swelling sun and rain,

And so shared with the poet who stole your lines
the anonymous birth of poetry,
the all or nothing of your torment
which you, unlettered pauper of the word
drew from the white invalid breast
the glittering word, thread of the airy web
of breath to breath,
soul to soul,
stone to stone.

The Bearded Men

I raise a flag of beards
Against the bald Caesars.

Nimbus of hoary heads
Rising like ruins vined,
Like the webbed and moss-hung tree,

Aloft in the schoolboy's awe,
Brooding in the scholar's dream,
The fine strands in the steel engraved,
In the meshed shadows grained.
Curled at the talmud reader's cheek,
The blond ruff gracing the armored breast,
The bright brushed hero's beard
Circling the rosy lip and joyous eye,
Lear's banner torn in the storm,
And Will's beard dawning on the briny line.

Flag of the bearded company,
Starred with their eyes, set in a field of pallor:
Here the beard of Homer pointing the wind's way
To the sunstruck ships in full sail,
Here the drained Face with golden mane,
The lost world darkening in the olive trees.
Here the robed prophet by his flocks,
Here iron browed Karl whose locks
Roll like a thundercloud,
Here gray-lipped Abe
Gazing from the shadowed eye.

And here the bearded boy lying in Spain,
One with the burning grass,
Crumbling to powdered loam,
Fouled and drying on the foreign sand.
And here the shaggy lad in Israel,
Flashing the deaths-head grin,
Cursing the hand that dropped the shell,
The field forsaken, the twig without a leaf,
The cicada shell, empty of all,
Open to the rain and moonbeam.

In What Land

In the first verse of the Tao
You, too, Laotzu, speak of words,
Of the source and end of words.
And a breath or two suffice you
To draw being and non-being
From the white page, a brimming lake,
Flowing cool for all to drink.

Where is that garden,
In what village, in what land,
Where you made Confucius wonder,
Where your guest is at home
With the sign of life in your face,
So boundless and so good,
Where your brother, long since descended
From a countryman of Jesus,
A plain man learning peace,
Is not confronted by fearful, wolfish men,
Each priest-marked with a sign of death,
And is not accused, tormented, and then destroyed?

Good Morning

How do you do, my learned friend,
How goes it, and how well do you intend?

Tell me you are a hardy friend of man,
A wary seeker in a silent art,
Tempered in the ethic of the song,
To draw the heart intact and weigh
The unborn tear, awake among the rest

In the historic night
By sorrow manifest.

Not quite, my friend so wry in heart,
Yours is the more genial part,
Skilled to comply, condone, contend,
And never dream, dear sir,
How you offend.

What's His Name

Poor butt of the hard glance,
the idle glance that knows you not
and cannot say
how it had ever ailed or failed
and when it does will moan
in a silly way.

Passing down the street, yes it was he,
the nightmare brow, face of tobacco ash,
hugging his papers, all his earthly goods
tight in his arm, and as we turned,
and from a mile away,
his eyes like tiny stars
twinkled in mine.

Greeting Card

Old Walt's sparkling head
Echoes afar,
His words like frosty dew
Scattering daylight.

I cry back my cracked laugh,
I send you this greeting card,
This bit of paper twirling in the air,
Inked with a prayer.
Answer, old man, are you there?

Voyage

Whitehead dares the atomic sea,
Sails the ciphered constellation,
Rounds the sphere of cosmic fear
To the dizzy correlation.

Steers by Einstein's stellar clocks,
Clears the philosophic rocks,
Follows the oceanic rhyme
Of the reason's space and time

And gathers on an utmost beach
What the sea-turned shell expounds
From the pulsing atom's skies,
Till the choral ear resounds.

Citizen

Hairless beast in old clothes
Dry-eyed, whispering as he moved:
Forty years paying the rent
Sending the boy to school
Saying amen, voting for president,
Gone with a tremor of the lip.

In the half octave of his sound
A hundred words, to pass the time of day
And thirty ciphers
To count his change and make his way
But not one word to tell his tale
Or hear the meaning of his name:
Or mark him once, whose warm cloaked heart
Played with all its might a little chime
While in the weed topped skull
The protean lenses turned to slime.

Look

You hide your tail and hoof,
And sweat and smile.

Bound by ciphers in a book
Added up by men of guile:
The monks of rent
And graven document.

By the argument sublime
They subtract your bread and roof,
And by the shining proof
And the distinction drawn so fine,
Whisk away your silk and wine,
And stand aloof.

Silly Bird

Man is the silliest bird,
Bedazzled by a word,
Twittering and absurd,
Tricked in a puff of air.
How he falls into the snare,
Hooked by the pen-scratch and the sign,
Like the hen on the chalk line!

Lord, what a fraud is Gawd!
Beware the primeval Order
And the universal Warder,
Minerva perfect from the brow,
Mind frozen from grace,
The stream of Time, the dream of Space,
The ultimate Base.
You get so vast about the Past
And lose your sense in the Immense.

Big shots, giants of the earth
Were meant for mirth.

When it is put so pat
That the Unknown is This and That,
Put on your hat.

A word like Intuition
Will lead you to perdition.

The mystic fire
Is a famous liar.

Heavenly Perfection
Pales in terror of correction:

If you touch her lovely wreath,
Draws a knife and bares her teeth.

Wordbound

The Greek, seabound, skybound,
Wordbound, saw himself enclosed,
And the enclosed within the enclosed,
Entailed within the entailed,
Drawn to an ever-farther Greece
Within the mirror of the mirror,
All in the noun's golden lineage,
The parallel into eternity,
From son to father and to father's father,
Thence to the final Parent, there to rest.

His spearpoint in the ground of time,
He stood unmoved, paced off a single stride,
And small and near, held fast the word of air,
To sum the image to the image,
The sun's avowal, the shade's dissent,
The angled temple, cool and square.

Icon

The image of mankind
Murdered and then maligned.

The word Arise was in his eyes,
He never told a man to kneel.
The raging wound won't heal,
The head will hang askew,
Until you learn that word Arise,
And rising lift him from his pain.
And then the mild young jew
Will walk again.

The Fault

Here it is in black and white,
The old chinaman sitting in the road
Where his son and daughter lie bleeding.
The boy and the girl must die.
And we must hear the siren and the falling glass,
The pavement will have to rise,
The braided wires twang apart
At the Bell Telephone Hour,
The door will have to fly wide
And the pillar leap
To make it clear beyond a doubt.
The iron vault
Must sink in the fault.
The books must soar like birds
And the window frame
Must flame and crackle in the universal tongue,
To show you what it's all about:
What was wrong
In the reason, in the song,
That broke the water main and blew the fuse,
That brought him to the charred road
And cracked the old man's heart.

Fear

In sad old dogma all is dreamed.
So tell me how this dream were cast
And from what being streamed.

I see the living millions stroll
Bright in the day before the blast
(The cloud is yet to roll)

Still in the noon of beauty swarm,
Yet stricken like the imaged past,
And blanched as in the storm.

So tell me, in what sight, what sleep
They walk undone, the lost, the last,
How the seeming, where the blunder

And say if none is there to weep
And seek the theme within the thunder.

Airborne

The happy fields, and then the sea
    Shot with the wakes of ships

Sudden and still like comets under
    My space-stained wing.

Think what has vanished there
    How clouds and men billow in time

And bear this height
    As I ascend like the sun,

Between me and my house a gulf
    And a fogged continent.

Brimming from the world's edge,
    The mirror-lands of my self,

My light and shade,
    Borne off as others are,

Where I have no fame,
    Where all mankind is without fame,

Without a sign but for this
    Gaunt winged intruder

(With me its secret in its hollow frame)
    Sounding on, in surfs of light.

I looked until we lost the world.
    Clouds were our only birds.

Prisoners of space!
    Though it turn to rock and then vapor,

Being is being. And my anxious wing
    Is constant to my end: to shine in distance

And never sink to my life down there
    In the past under a fog.

I am the angel that the ancients knew,
    In their old minds I rang

To stand in heaven's sight
    And know the face of the world.

History

The rock did not know the mountain
And the leaf did not know the tree
But man beheld mankind
And told his history,

And asked, who knows the world?
And answered, he who weeps.
Dante heard the moan
Known to citizens of hell,
To them alone,
Known to Lenin and to Blake,
In Shelley's heart awake,
Beating in the city heat
Weaving England's winding sheet.

China, India, translate!
Write it for tomorrow's text.
All the smiling clerks of hate
And engineers of hunger wait
To know it next. The eyelid wet
 (America will know it yet)
Stains the balance sheet of state.

Art

With a bit of earth ground fine
And a tuft of sable hair,
Decide the land and sea
On a linen square
Or sheet of pine,
Dispose the day and night
And read the rhymes of light.

Yellow, red and blue,
Enough for false and true.
A string drawn tight
Will do for wrong and right,
A brassy bell, a grassy reed,
To sound all hell
And the world's need.

The Outer Land

1

I heard the noisy prophets
In a barbarous tongue,
And I sought out the soft spoken alien,
In a cobbler's apron, grinding a lens,
And by his glass I saw another earth and air,
At the snowy peak the sun's rim, sphered in night,
And the night's face again in light unknown.
And through another eye and yet another,
Journeyed the atom's odyssey,
Back to my island home.

2

The seaborn with the wave in torment tossed,
Fall to the shore, gasp in the rarer sea,
Swarm to the wave of sand.

The black weed, stiffened on the rock,
Greens and swells in the flooding tide
And blooms in glory;
And the desert seed is caught
Beside the solitary spring
And there is wooed to life.

So each to being dawns,
Enters the heaven of being,
Held close and loved awhile,
And basks in the heaven of being,
And cleaves to being and weeps for being,
Grazes in fields of being,
On being feeding and to being reaching,
By being slain, from heaven gone.

3

The human omnivore
By few is ever seen,
Goes singly in the swarm,
Consuming all, prowls by the lighted eye,
Rises and falls by sight,
Misreads the sign
In his own vista by his dark intent
And stalks the other, to the other strives
And eats alone, and lonely cries.

And cry to cry becomes the choir of night,
(As leaf to leaf the forest shade)
The sound of sounds, that mankind makes.

Word

You that have known and will no more
know but be known, mourned, lost
in a wave of other sound,
while none can guess
what whisked you from their day and night,
endure merely by that same death
which turned your thirst into a word,
your figure in the air upon the land
into a fading script, committed
to a memory that will pass in turn
from seeing to being, from
scheming to seeming:
assenting in the denial,
vague in the certainty,
bright in the gloom
of any word,
sounded in its quiet and quiet,
alive for death and dead.

Idle Noon

Benign old face with sinister marks,
heavy cat gorged and battered,
its sweet sleep covered with a scowl,
who yawned to simulate indifference
while bright venoms scaled the cheeks,
it is the mind that rides him,

bearing south to the Avenue
of brave breasts and bright-shod feet;
it is that angry gong
which strikes its only note
at every blow.

The night air does the trick,
draws on his jaws their tiny hebrew tune;
above the quaint lament,
his mind, a cautious moon,
discovers happiness:
his glow, that had survived
that moon's exhausting guess,
and reached its idle noon.

Since He Must

I saw him wandering down a street,
and thought: perhaps there are some
who are glad that his luminous head
moves under the sun and moon.

That harsh knot with a halo of flesh,
with dark moths eating his cheeks,
that wind-bitten tentacle
shrunken to a fist.

I saw him sneaking down the street,
robed in someone else's rags.
What was a mouse doing in his heart
and why when his big hands might strangle it
did they search instead for crumbs?
To learn and know
his bones aghast; since he must burn
he would burn slow.

Gallant

A woman tiptoed at his side on tiny
black hoofs; from wall to wall she hopped,
her heart a little fife of shrills and screams.

Once in a grove
he was born, and leered,
bare in the air, without heat,
peeled peach, weak sun,
stripped onion, bleeding beet.
Once he stood looking from behind
when his face slipped to one side
showing only half his eye,
his soul a gaze
holding his face before.
In a dark room he wore
the naked eye turning on his hours.

Dangling feet kiss wooden floor
and he in wrath gasps small and reedy,
weeps while his beloved cowers.

Street

Night street, yielding to light,
telling the heart
it is the same as rock, skull, moon:
yielding a yawn of its own stuff,
when ground by wheels of iron and air,
and hinting
of that harshness without rhetoric
which drama seeks, forever failing

with things that warm and bleed;
sneer of steel that is to the touch
what it is to the sun;
most secret when most bare.
At the verge of its voice,
his fears outroar his hearing,
to keep his ears intact awhile.

Diary

Two women hurried past.
I would follow them
but they would bite if I touched them.

An auto hissed them round the corner,
shooed from a fevered mind,
blared from the vacant night,
escaped around the corner.

I fell into a cafeteria,
I leaned on a little rectangle,
making a design I could not see
in the mirror behind me.

Men in neat shrouds sat aslant,
killed by this flypaper cafeteria,
their elbows stirred,
their hats slipped various ways.